MILES

maglificio   italiano lana   e   seta

Edited by
Cristina Beltrami

Marsilio Arte

Cover
Shantung and madras outfit, 1979, detail

pp. 1-4, 213-216, endpapers
Departments at the Miles plant, Vicenza, 2024

Translations
Cristina Popple

Graphic design and layout
Carmen Malafronte

Copy editing
Elisabetta Righes

© 2024 by Miles s.p.a.
© 2024 by Marsilio Arte® s.r.l., Venice

First edition September 2024
ISBN 979-12-5463-239-0

Photo Credits
Unless otherwise noted, all photos by
    Enrico Fiorese
pp. 14, 15, 17-21, 23, 27, 32-33, 43, 56, 59, 62,
    65-66, 68, 72, 79-80, 82, 86, 88, 90, 105-106,
    111-112, 132, 137, 204-208: Archivio Storico
    Bocchese
pp. 14 (bottom left), 40: Archivio Vaienti, Vicenza
pp. 24-25: ph Ilvio Gallo / © Galleria Borghese,
    Rome
p. 76: © Duc, Léna Kordic / *Elle* France
p. 85: © Arthur Elgort, Francine Vormese, Nicole
    Crassat / *Elle* France
p. 92: *Marie Claire* France
p. 97: ph Gilles Bensimon
p. 108: ph Ilvio Gallo / © Palazzo Corsini, Florence
p. 179: ph Ilvio Gallo
p. 209: Maison Alaïa

Our sincerest thanks to
Sandra Backlund
Gilles Bensimon
Maria Vittoria Bocchese
Lison Bonfils
Orsola de Castro
Fondation Azzedine Alaïa
Ilvio Gallo
Maison Alaïa
Pieter Mulier
Anna Orioles
Sophie Théallet
Renzo Zengiaro

*To all of Miles' employees—past, present
and future*

Contents

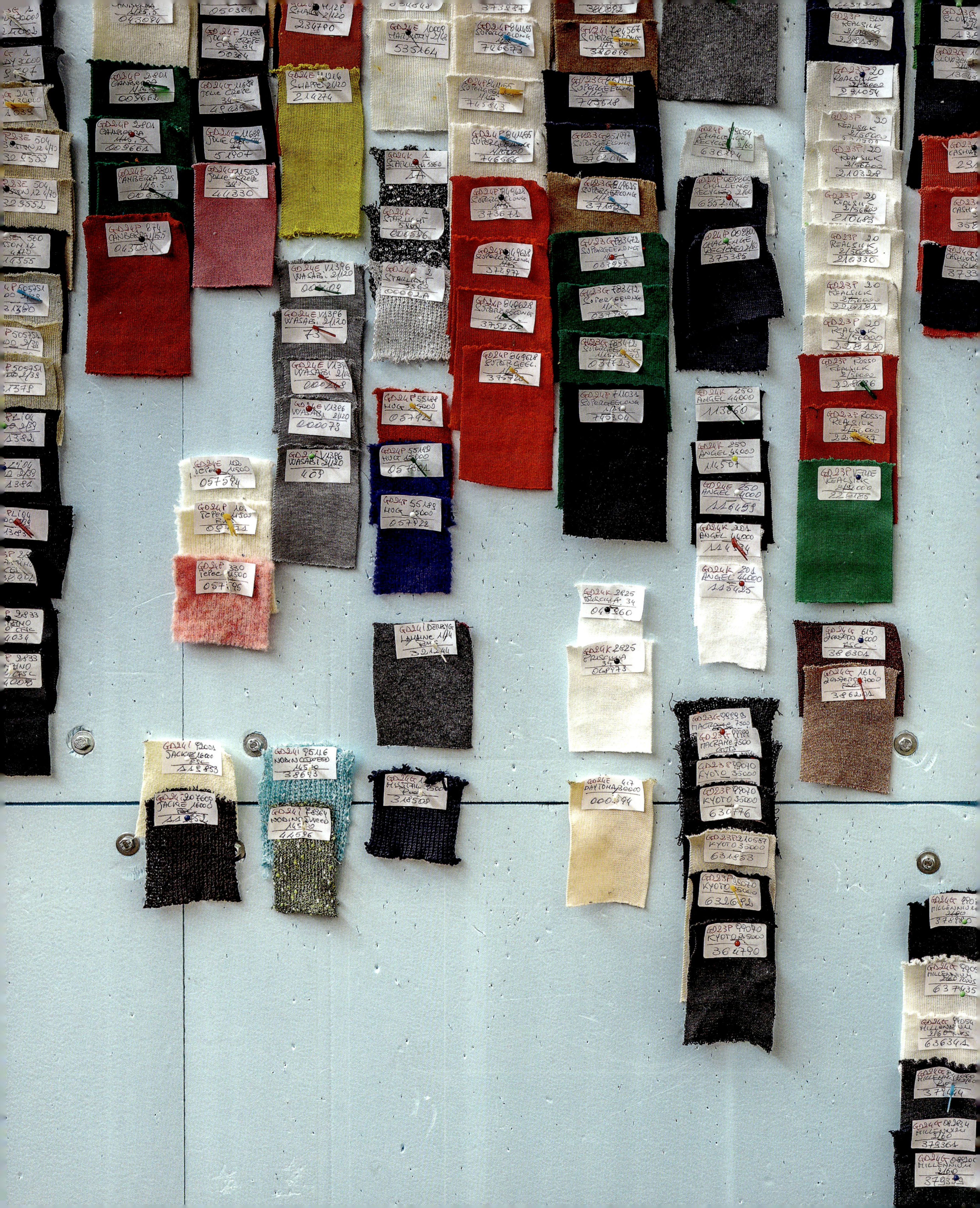

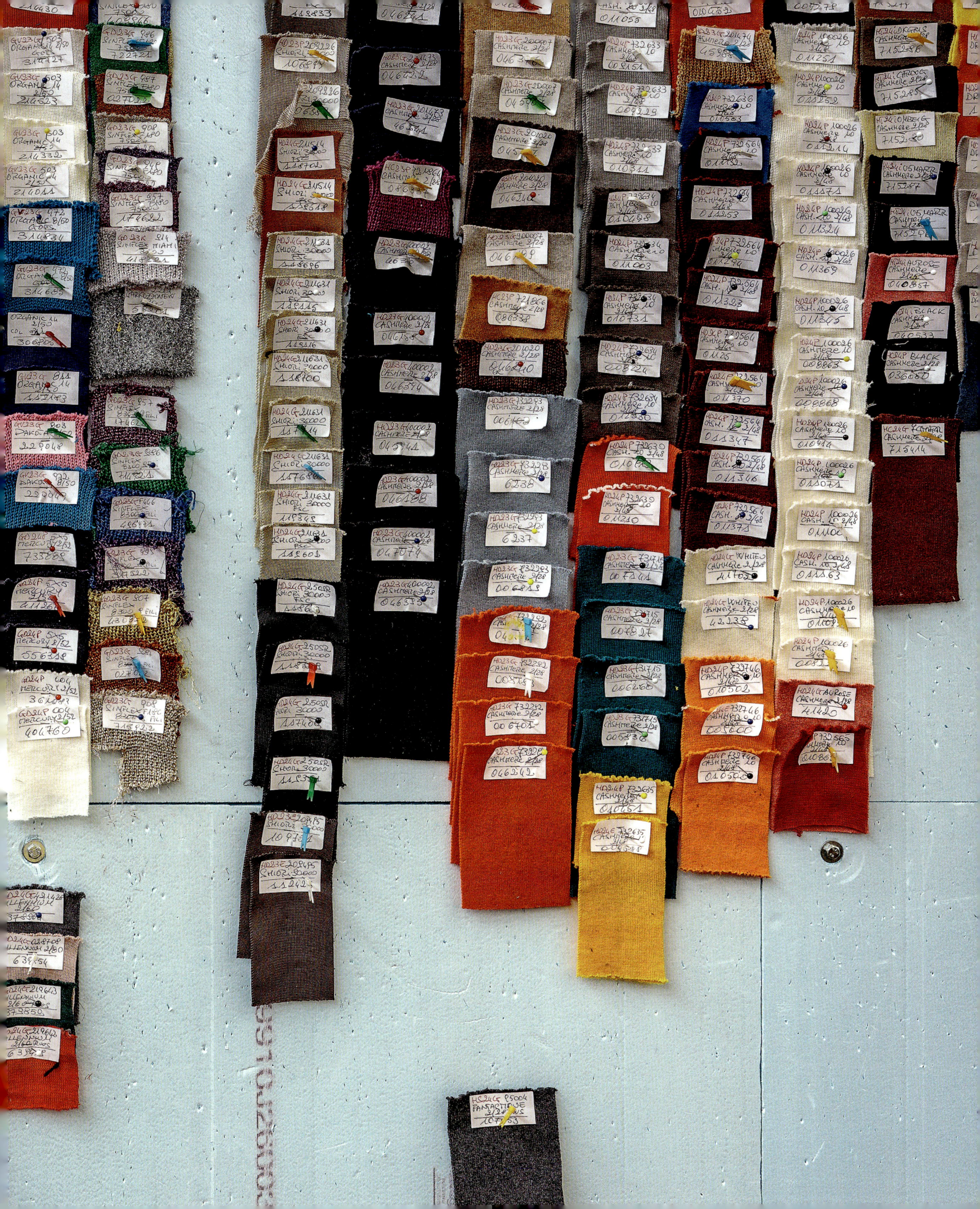

Introduction

Pieter Mulier

Miles was there with Alaïa always, from the beginning, and it remains. Like a heartbeat. A special bond we have both created and cherished. Of course, I think of Silvia Bocchese, who founded Miles. She was the first to understand what Azzedine desired and who knew how to help Alaïa transform into a major fashion house by offering all her expertise and devotion. She forged such strong ties between Vicenza and Paris that the professional relationship turned into a friendship. This is the strongest, most sincere proof of the unique bond that exists between us.

Miles has supported and collaborated with Azzedine since the outset. And when I joined Alaïa, I could pursue the quest for radical and innovative beauty and timeless excellence. With the same trust and freedom, the same unique bond.

Miles welcomed me like a lifelong friend who is allowed to ask everything. With each collection, I can take all the risks. Create without limits, supported by Miles' haute craftsmanship. Continue what Azzedine had started: unique creations in knitwear that are part of the essence of the House, shaping its silhouette. Reinventing the possibilities of knitwear.

In the late 1970s, Azzedine Alaïa asked Miles to produce a bodysuit for a belt—two pieces that went on to become emblematic of the Alaïa wardrobe. This marked the beginning of an uninterrupted relationship. Miles became part of Alaïa's close circle, its family—an idea so dear to Azzedine and rooted in the essence of the Maison.

It is thanks to the unique know-how, techniques, and expertise of Miles that Alaïa was able to develop its iconic knitwear. This endless quest for innovation and creation is based on a dialogue between Miles and Alaïa. For a creator, it is a privilege to engage in such a relationship. Every idea, even the most ambitious, becomes achievable.

I think back to the collection inspired by Picasso's Tanagras: thanks to Miles, the knit was able to reproduce the shapes, colors, and movements of the original sculptures. Knit became an infinite field of possibilities. One of our latest collections started from a single strand of merino wool, developed and reinvented with Miles. Reduced to its essential form, knit became the foundation of all creations.

Both Alaïa and Miles are committed to excellence. This shared vision ensures that every creation is not only a product of superior craftsmanship but also a testament to a mutual passion for quality and artistry. A shared devotion to perfection and beauty.

"It all seemed normal to me: I was working"

Cristina Beltrami interviews Silvia Bocchese

Celebrating its first sixty years of activity in 2022, Maglificio italiano lana e seta (Miles) is inextricably tied to the figure of its founder, Silvia Stein Bocchese.

Born in Zurich on January 19, 1939, Silvia Stein spent her early childhood in German-speaking Switzerland, where alongside the usual school curriculum she also took ballet lessons. In 1948, the family moved to Schio (Vicenza), where her father, an engineer, was the director of De Pretto-Escher Wyss. Thus, that summer Silvia started studying Italian for up until then all of her schooling had been in German, and in the fall she started fourth grade in Schio. After her early experiences in Italian schools, she decided to further her knowledge of languages by taking French classes at the Florissant pension in Lausanne and by spending some months in London, where she stayed with an aunt who offered her the opportunity to fully experience the freedom of Swinging London.

Upon returning to Schio, she started working for her father as his personal secretary and soon, thanks to common friends, she made the acquaintance of Giuseppe Bocchese, a textile entrepreneur from Vicenza[1], whom she married as soon as she came of age in February 1960.

Cristina Beltrami: You have recently shown me a photograph of yourself as little more than a newborn playing with a ball of yarn. What did you think when you saw it?

Silvia Bocchese: I found it amusing. I don't see predestination in it, but I remember that as a child I was always holding a ball of yarn. In fact, I had two or three and I played with them.

I favored angora and I've been told that one time, on the train between Zurich and Bern, I was trying to pull the threads out of the puffy sweater worn by the woman sitting next to me.

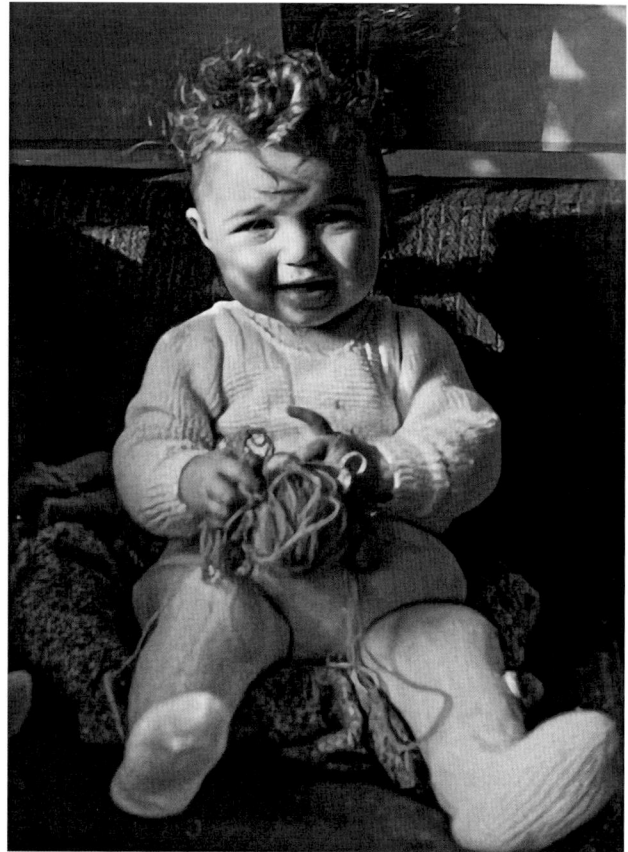

Cristina Beltrami interviews Silvia Bocchese

CB: And what do you feel when you observe the aerial shot taken in 1960 of the new Giuseppe Bocchese & Figli plant out in the middle of nowhere, surrounded only by the Venetian countryside?

SB: It takes me back to the day of its inauguration. I remember perfectly well when the ribbon of the new silk factory was cut in 1960. It was a state-of-the-art establishment at the time. Mariano Rumor, then Minister for Agriculture and also from Vicenza, was in attendance. But I also remember the rows upon rows of incredibly modern looms, the brand new offices: just think that this table where we are having our chat, just like those cabinets over there and the chairs, are still the same as that day.
It's true, the factory was surrounded by fields, and no one could imagine such a rapid growth.

CB: Are the beginnings of Miles also connected to silk?

SB: Yes, my husband managed the family company, which had been producing woven silk fabric for men's clothing since 1908. At the time, men wore elegant silk suits, often paired with shirts that were also made of silk. I loved those iridescent threads; I especially liked shantung because it inevitably contained knots, imperfections. So I tried using it to produce some samples of knit silk, which no one was making at the time.

CB: What did you feel in your own workshop in 1962, aged twenty-three, with your three workers? What kind of atmosphere was it?

SB: We had a very strong, collaborative relationship. We worked together with enthusiasm and few questions asked, especially about the future. Our roles weren't really defined: we all did a bit of everything. For example, I took care of deliveries, too, or mod-

"It all seemed normal to me: I was working"

eled my own pieces. I couldn't replace the people working the machines: at the time they were manual and you needed technical training I was lacking.
Sometimes I wonder why I had this fixation with knitwear. It would have been much easier if I'd produced clothes using woven silk fabric.

CB: How did one conquer the French brands from Vicenza in the 1960s?

SB: I must thank Lison Bonfils for my French debut. She already knew Giuseppe, and she worked in fashion in both Italy and France. Towards the end of the 1960s, Lison set up a meeting with Monsieur Yves Saint Laurent, who had recently opened a prêt-à-porter boutique. I started out creating some garments for him and, later on, Miles became the licensee for the brand Saint Laurent Rive Gauche. Our contract with Céline was a consequence of this collaboration. In fact, in Cannes there was a boutique that sold items by both Yves Saint Laurent and Céline, who was just then expanding their production beyond the narrow confines of leather goods. Richard Vipiana, Madame Céline's husband, came to Vicenza and asked me to produce some pieces for their brand, for which we later became licensees.
I usually met with Madame Céline Vipiana in Milan, where she would give me instructions regarding the production of the garments, which were mostly very classic in style: their iconic piece was a cardigan with gold buttons that we produced for several consecutive seasons.

CB: In 1962 you already had children: how did you manage your time between family and work?

SB: I was undoubtedly able to do what I did because I could count on my husband's intelligence and sensitivity, and on the presence of my mother. On the one hand, in fact, Giuseppe understood how important my job was to me and he supported me: he didn't prevent my leaving for days in a row, often taking the night train for Rome or Paris, leaving our four children at home with their grandmother. I think this was quite exceptional in Italy at the time.
Of course, it weighed on me to leave my family, but I love my work and I tried to get my children interested from a very early age: they came to the factory, played with the distaffs, saw me fiddling around with sketches and samples, or discussing things.

CB: What was travel like at the time?

SB: I enjoyed traveling by train, though there were a few "particular" episodes. At the time, we still had customs and the inspections could be extremely thorough. I remember this one time when I was traveling with a suitcase full of prototypes for a Saint Laurent fashion show, and I hadn't had the time to prepare the paperwork because then, as now, time was always short before a *défilé*. At the border crossing they awoke me in the dead of night and asked me to get out of the carriage for a luggage check. I didn't have enough cash to pay the fine and I had to wait in a waiting room for the money to come through the next day so I could leave. I had a large truffle in my purse, which they luckily hadn't found during the inspection, so when I got to Paris that evening I dined on egg and truffle with Lison and her husband Didier.

CB: When did you understand that the French market was the market for you?

SB: It might have been then, between the 1960s and the 1970s. After all, fashion was French at the time—it spoke almost exclusively French, a language I luckily knew very well. I had Valentino in Rome, but my main clients were in Paris. I sometimes ended up spending three nights in a row in a sleeping car: from Vicenza to Paris, from Paris to Rome, and then I took the night train home from the capital.

CB: What did it mean to work in fashion in Paris in the 1960s and '70s?

SB: It was an extraordinary city with a wonderful energy, and it still is, all in all. But it seems to me that everything was more within reach at the time: we had a direct relationship with the designers. Lison was a precious access key for me: after Saint Laurent, she had introduced me to Gaby Aghion from Chloé, one of the first brands, possibly the very first, to design luxury prêt-à-porter. We worked very well with them for years. These were professional relationships that often became something more: we had lunch together, we chatted about stuff not related to work. It was thanks to Lison that I met Azzedine Alaïa, too: we were friends, we hung out, we often went to his house. He was nice. At first, I didn't even think we would work together.
At the time, Chloé's designer was Karl Lagerfeld, who visited Vicenza quite often. Once, it must have been the very early '80s, he was here at Miles and I mentioned that I had

16

↓ Karl Lagerfeld, addressed envelope
   and sketch (pen, marker, and colored
   pencil on paper) for a Carnival costume
   for Silvia Bocchese, circa 1980

been invited to Venice for a Carnival ball. He made no comment at the time, but after two days I received an envelope with a wonderful design and a letter with the detailed instructions for the creation of a knit costume.

CB: In 1980, Miles was devastated by a terrible fire that destroyed everything, even the machines: but you didn't give up.

SB: Yes, the fire destroyed everything. I remember I spent one whole sleepless night thinking, and then I followed my instinct, which was to carry on even though everyone said I should give up. With the help of the firemen, my son Alessandro had managed to salvage a box containing a few garments, the prototypes for a Chloé collection, and I took them to Paris where they were modeled on the catwalk. At that point, Miles moved into the center of Vicenza, to a much smaller space where I worked with ten workers and the few manual machines that the mechanics had managed to repair. Then there was another episode that gave me great faith at the time: one client, a foreigner, understood my situation and helped me out by paying me in advance for the thread I would need to produce his order.

That was also when my providential collaboration with Alaïa began.

CB: Could you tell us about how this professional relationship began and later turned into a real friendship?

SB: In the late 1970s, I got a phone call from Lison Bonfils who asked me to quickly produce a bodysuit for a belt that Alaïa had created for Charles Jourdan—an unusual accessory, a sort of mini *panier* made of cord bordered in leather—which had to be photographed for an *Elle* editorial. I made the bodysuit and Lison took it to Paris. There it was photographed by Nicole Crassat and published with clear indications of where it could be purchased, that is to say at Azzedine's house in rue de Bellechasse, where I had left fifty or so pieces. They were all different colors because I was in such a hurry that I used whatever yarn I had on hand.

After that idea, it all went very fast. Lison produced a few sketches of knit garments for her friend Azzedine who immediately took to them: they were sweaters, mostly black, ribbed, viscose and cotton for the summer, cashmere and wool for the winter. We then created leggings and women loved them. In 1981, Mirabelle Saint-Marie, a brilliant commercial director, left Thierry Mugler and became Alaïa's right-hand woman. At the same time, we were licensed to produce and distribute his brand.

CB: How did you communicate with Alaïa in the 1980s? I'm talking about defining the styles.

SB: Alaïa worked with paper patterns: he was a veritable tailor, a knitwear sculptor of sorts.

I would ship lengths of knit fabric produced following his exact instructions to him in Paris. He created the garment using a model and then made a paper pattern that he sent back to Vicenza. A few days later he arrived in person, generally accompanied by the model Zuleika Ponsen, his dog Patapouf, and an assistant. We set to work. We all had dinner together and often Azzedine continued to work afterwards: he was a real perfectionist.

In time, we added a guest house designed by our friend Flavio Albanese. Sonia Rykiel also spent a lot of time there designing and working, surrounded by the peace of the Colli Berici. It was a different approach to work.

CB: What do you remember today of Sonia Rykiel and how she expressed her creativity?

SB: Sonia Rykiel was capable of transposing her idea of a garment into a sketch that was very easy to interpret. Well, unlike Azzedine who used a mannequin for his creations, she used sketches. And above all, for her knitwear was a fundamental element in a collection. I began working with her towards the end of the 1980s and our professional understanding developed into a friendship. She was an extremely ironic woman and her collections were a mirror of this endearing aspect of her character.

CB: Are there workers who have always been with Miles?

SB: The first that comes to mind is "Impossible," as Alaïa called her, because if he asked for anything that went beyond the norm, her answer was invariably "it can't be done"; but then she always came through.

↗ The guesthouse designed by Flavio Albanese
in the Colli Berici in 1989

More recently, we've had a programmer who didn't speak a word of French and yet had a perfect understanding with Alaïa: he would show her a piece of cloth, she would study its structure, and as soon as she got back to Vicenza she would reproduce it in knit.

CB: When did you understand that your professional relationship with Alaïa would be crucial for Miles?

SB: I think it was as early as the 1980s, for sure at the New York fashion show in 1982 where he presented a huge number of knit pieces, a trend he never reversed. And above all, Azzedine never considered it an accessory: he understood knitwear, he knew how to interrogate it and obtain magnificent results, even when it came to haute couture.

CB: Then, in the 2000s, Carla Sozzani became a part of your relationship with Alaïa, is that right?

SB: Yes, in more recent years Carla Sozzani followed Alaïa closely, they had a very strong understanding. Azzedine himself would say: "C'est la femme la plus intéressante d'Italie."[2]
Consequently, I found myself working side by side with Carla, too, and together we have overcome very complex professional challenges while establishing a relationship of reciprocal respect and friendship. Working together can create a powerful connection—when it works.

CB: For at least one decade now, Miles has also been producing home apparel collections: would you tell us about the "Miles Home" adventure?

SB: In the 1990s, I decided to make cashmere blankets to give a number of clients as gifts. I remember I made a large blanket bordered with a gold motif for Madame Rykiel, and I realized there was a demand for this product. So I began to study the luxury blanket

market as a whole and decided to produce some with our own brand that my son Nicola and I presented in 1997 at Heimtextil, the textile fair in Frankfurt.

The uniqueness of these blankets lay not only in the quality of the yarn but also in the technique: I didn't want the hem to be applied but rather I wanted it to be part of a single operation of the machine.

I brought my designer friend Flavio Albanese into the "Home" adventure, too. He is from Vicenza, like us, and has designed some jacquard motifs for the collection.

> **CB:** Speaking of people from Vicenza, you were present when the brand Bottega Veneta was launched overseas.

SB: The founders of the label, Michele Taddei and Renzo Zengiaro, were friends of my husband's, and when they decided to try to conquer the US market and open a boutique that bore their name on Madison Avenue—which wasn't the fancy street it is today—the girls and I went with them, in part because we were curious, but also to encourage them and because they trusted our taste. We were present for the set-up of the boutique, designed to look like a corner of Venice in New York—it was a great adventure!

> **CB:** Do you believe that a company like Miles is in part the result of the industrial fabric of Vicenza? Let me explain: aside from the undeniable economic boom of the 1960s, do your think an undertaking such as yours would have been possible in a less industrialized area?

SB: No, Miles is deeply rooted in Veneto, and specifically in the area of Vicenza. Our organization is typical of this district: the designing is all done in house, and we collaborate with a number of extremely specialized workshops in the production phase.

Luckily, our country has been able to preserve most of its fashion industry and this sets us apart from other European countries. You could say that luxury knitwear is produced for the most part in Italy. I still remember the huge blue bags that left the company headed for the houses of the workers who worked from home.

This tight-knit network of highly specialized craftspeople is typical of some areas of Italy and sets us apart from the rest of Europe. France, for example, once had a similar industrial system, small and widespread, but it no longer exists.

> **CB:** Were you ever tempted to create your own label? Not even at the beginning?

SB: No. I've never been creative, but I was interested in materializing the desires of creatives, of taking up the challenge and finding the best possible solution, creating artisanal products on an industrial level.

> **CB:** What did you feel when you saw Alaïa's pieces exhibited in museums such as Galleria Borghese or Palais Galliera in Paris?

↘ Silvia Bocchese, Paola Agostoni,
Renzo Zengiaro, and Laura Moltedo
on Madison Avenue scouting for a location
for the first Bottega Veneta boutique
in New York, 1972

"It all seemed normal to me: I was working"

"Like Silvia, I always experienced that moment
in the first person, the moment of 'creation,'
where everything was possible. Quite simply,
if you had initiative, the will to work hard...
you would succeed. And if you were good,
you would soon emerge.
[...] We were all friends, nice people,
in the company of beautiful young women
who were the embodiment of Italian good taste
and elegance; we were a team, so to speak!"

Renzo Zengiaro, Vicenza, January 2023

↑   Some of Alaïa's most iconic pieces
at the show *Azzedine Alaïa. Couture/
Sculpture* at Galleria Borghese, Rome, 2015

SB: It has always elicited powerful emotions! Especially the exhibition at Galleria Borghese, which we visited with the entire staff from Miles. It was wonderful to share with my collaborators the surprise of seeing the garments we had produced surrounded by the beauty of the sculptures and the other works at Villa Borghese. I remember that the guides enjoyed questioning the workers, who knew everything about those beautiful pieces of clothing.
Their reaction was touching: they were proud, they recognized the pieces, they remembered the difficulties, every detail they had had to finish by hand… That was very possibly the best moment.

CB: Are other pieces you have worked on present in museums?

SB: Yes, with Sandra Backlund we developed a series of garments that presented a real technical challenge, the fruit of in-depth research that ferried knitwear into the field of pure sculpture, and it's only fitting that they can now be found in the fashion collections at the MET in New York.

CB: When you began your cooperation with Orsola de Castro, it was the very early years of green fashion: what did you see in her that made you instantly believe in her?

SB: Actually, Orsola de Castro was my daughter's discovery: Bettina brought her to Vicenza and I trusted her quite simply because she had a beautiful idea. I liked the thought of using materials leftover from production that would thus be able to have a second life, becoming unique and colorful garments; having a cooperative of disabled people produce them only made the entire operation more beautiful.

CB: What has it meant to you to receive important acknowledgements such as the Talents du luxe et de la création prize in 2018 or the Cavalierato del lavoro in 2020?

SB: I was surprised and at the same time I was very happy, because the Talents is a prize created by the world of French fashion, which is extremely demanding, and having our President acknowledge my accomplishments was very moving for me as an Italian citizen.

CB: The confidentiality of Miles' archive of stitches and garments is legendary: has it become more complicated to preserve their secrecy with today's technological developments?

SB: I began at a time when we sent sketches by mail and then by fax, when the garments were concealed until we reached the fashion show and at best someone who was good at drawing could steal the design as it went down the catwalk.
Today, images and ideas travel at great speed, but the same question is still at the heart of everything. It isn't so much a question of secrecy, but rather of loyalty towards our client: I have always tried to prevent Miles from producing garments that were similar to one another.

There have been cases when I refused to duplicate a stitch or a piece of clothing, which happened mainly when we started producing Alaïa's collections, with the result that I even lost a few clients.

CB: Do you miss the personal relationship with the designers?

SB: Yes, quite a bit, because for the most part they had very energetic and charming personalities; they were a constant stimulus to me, as were their closest collaborators, be they Loulou de La Falaise for Yves Saint Laurent or Consuelo Crespi for Mr. Valentino, and then there were Karl Lagerfeld and Giorgio Armani. We were licensees for Mr. Armani's main collection, both women's and men's, for twelve years, and we produced some extremely sophisticated knit items in which his style is immediately recognizable.

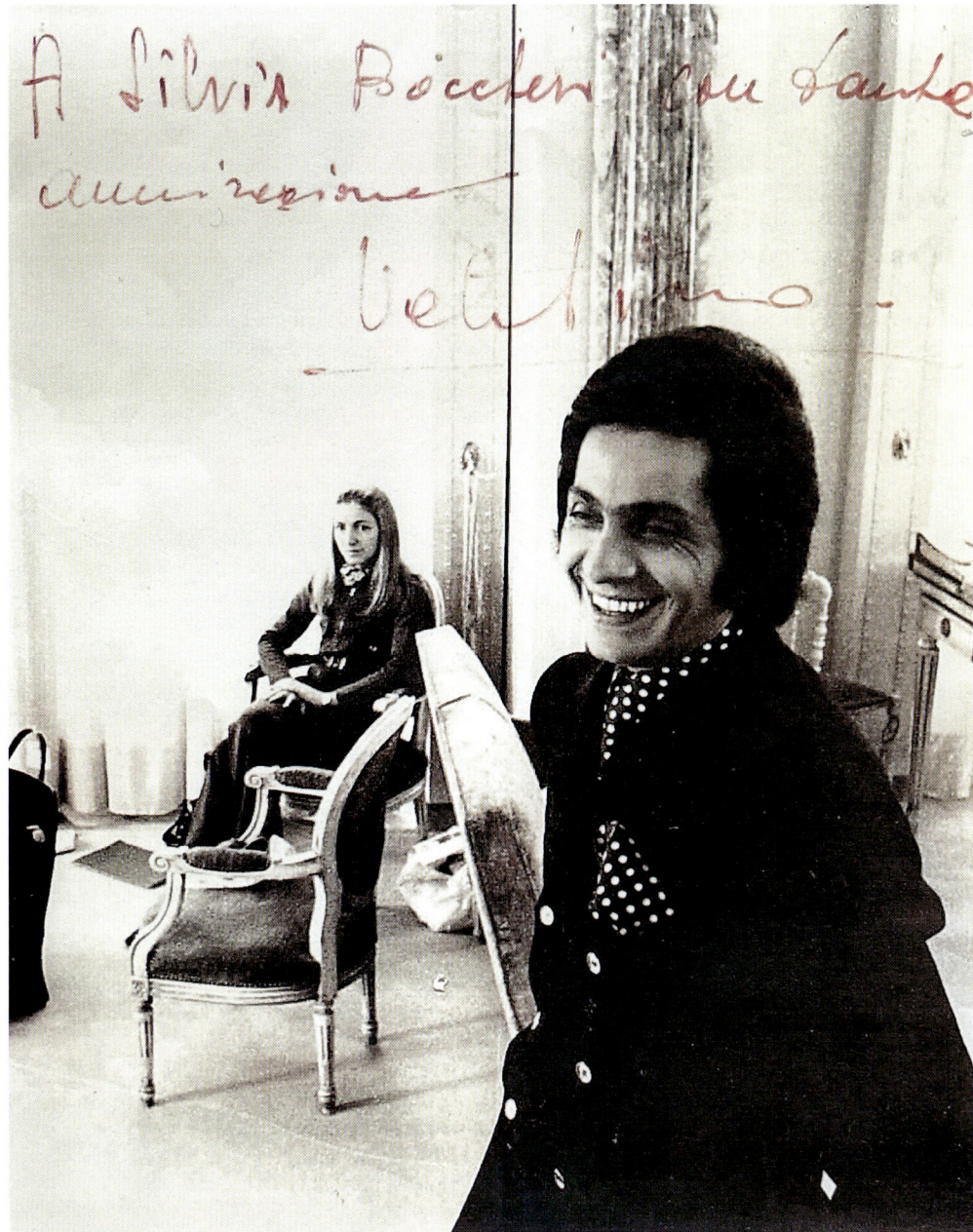

Not to mention Alaïa, with whom a direct and very close relationship meant spending entire days together, visiting shows and museums, late night calls, exchanges on the possibilities of knitwear…

CB: How do you feel about *A View to a Kill*, the 1985 episode of the James Bond saga starring Grace Jones sheathed in an Alaïa produced here in Vicenza?

SB: It makes me smile. I remember her and Alaïa together: they were friends, in 1987 she even went with him when he was awarded a prestigious Fashion prize by the French Ministry for Culture—in a knit dress, of course.
Another time, Azzedine begged us to produce the bodysuits for Tina Turner's choristers. The singer wore Alaïa herself and was going to hold a concert at the Arena in Verona. We produced them posthaste, and I delivered them myself to the artist's dressing room. She invited me backstage to watch the show: an unforgettable night, because of the complexity of such a production, which is something you can only discover by being backstage, and because of Turner's immense energy.

CB: What do you think of the boom of big chain stores selling low-cost clothing?

SB: They mirror the times exactly. In the 1970s and 1980s, there was something called a "total look": you wore clothes designed by the same person, from the same collection, while today people mix and match garments every which way. A "good" sweater over large-scale distribution pants—which after all gives women a great freedom of choice. Nowadays it's very difficult to connect a fashion line to the historical period we're living. In the past, we were also more bound to form: in the 1960s we made sure our shoes matched our purse when we went out for tea. Now people are freer, and this freedom is within everyone's financial reach, but with a huge cost in surplus that needs to be recycled somehow.

CB: In 2022, Miles produced a collection of garments inspired by Picasso's ceramics: sculpture-like clothes that were modeled on the catwalk and then exhibited at the Musée National Picasso in Paris like veritable works of art. Do you believe that such a close exchange between art and fashion is profitable?

SB: The cooperation with the Picasso Foundation was born from an idea of Pieter Mulier's, Alaïa's new creative director and an art connoisseur. He designed a series of sculpture-like garments inspired by the marvelous Tanagra ceramics produced by Picasso in the 1940s and 1950s. It is a visionary project, as magnificent as it was complex to create, for it isn't a mere graphic reproduction of a decoration or motif, but rather Pieter pursued a three-dimensional rendering, as if bringing the ceramics to life. It was a technical challenge and Miles emerged from it enriched. I believe this is one of the fundamental roles of great creators: leading us beyond what we perceive to be our limits.

CB: What future do you see for knitwear?

SB: I see a future of ups and downs, like for everything, but I believe it will always be an important branch of the clothing industry: it's not only beautiful, but also very comfortable. This branch depends greatly on the progress of technology: today knitting machines can do things that used to be unthinkable, and who knows what they might be able to do in the future. I believe knitwear will achieve a revolution of such depth that nothing in the textile industry will be comparable.

CB: Your children are now all working in the family business: how did the generational handover take place?

SB: They've always been involved, even when they were little, I would take them with me to Paris. Alessandro, my eldest, joined the company even before graduating because I needed someone to oversee administration. Nicola, my second, was interested in production from the very start. Michele, on the other hand, made his way as a consultant. He became the manager of another company and only joined the family business later on to follow the commercial side. Bettina has come on board just recently: her presence was crucial when I had to start cutting down on my business trips to Paris, and gradually she's started handling the development of the collections. All this happened very peacefully, naturally, possibly because I've always tried not to be too controlling. By observing the experiences of other business people, I realized that if a parent-figure is too strong, their children can perceive themselves as unfit, and so I strove for mine to act autonomously, sometimes even by stepping back.

1   The Giuseppe Bocchese & Figli silk factory was founded in 1908 by Giuseppe Bocchese senior and was later managed by his three sons, who chose to work in the family business: Giuseppe, Prospero, and Luciano. In its early days, the Giuseppe Bocchese & Figli plant in Trissino merely treated silk. It wasn't until 1928 that the company started twisting and weaving, later becoming specialized in the production of shantung.
2   Sozzani and Saillard 2022, 355 (the quote is from 2013).

It All Began with a Simple Pullover

Cristina Beltrami interviews Lison Bonfils

Lison Bonfils, muse, consultant, and creator of her own line, made her debut at the age of seventeen as a model for Dior and in 1958 became an editor for *Elle*.

Cristina Beltrami: How did you meet Silvia Bocchese?

Lison Bonfils: In the 1960s I collaborated with several groups in the Italian fashion industry. I also knew Giuseppe Bocchese, who told me about his young wife. They had children, but she also ran her own company. I visited her in her workshop in Vicenza, where I discovered a small machine used to make silk ties and a couple of knitting machines; I quickly produced two sketches, one for a silk marinière and the other for a cashmere crew neck with tiny embroidery.
I then took my sweaters to Paris, where Hélène Gordon-Lazareff immediately noticed them and wanted to photograph them for *Elle*. It was her idea to put Silvia Bocchese in touch with Yves Saint Laurent, who was opening his boutique on the Rive Gauche and needed some original pieces. A few years later, I was having dinner at the Café de Flore with Gaby Aghion, the creator of the Chloé brand, and I told her about Silvia and the Miles knitwear factory and how they were already working with Saint Laurent: this led to a fruitful collaboration that lasted many years.

CB: What was the Parisian fashion world like in the 1960s?

LB: Magnificent! That was the time when prêt-à-porter was born. We went from haute couture with its paper patterns sold to specialized seamstresses or the big US brands, to simpler garments designed for a younger audience who no longer wanted to wear expensive, bourgeoise clothes.

←   Silk organzine pullover and embroidered cashmere pullover, both designed by Lison Bonfils

CB: Looking specifically at knitwear, what was the situation in Europe at the time?

LB: If you observe the situation in Europe in the 1960s, you'll see that in Italy they only had hand machines that mimicked hand-knitting. Great Britain was famous for its cashmere and its shetland, but they kept repeating the same models. In France there was a huge industry producing worsted wool garments, but always in the canonical shapes: crew necks, turtle necks, vests. In Troyes they were specialized in jacquard and jersey. So, creating something different out of knitwear, and maybe even finding a new customer base, wasn't easy. Miles was very forward thinking when they chose to occupy that wedge of the market.

CB: You created your own collections, too—you even put Silvia Bocchese on the catwalk—and some knitwear with Miles: would you tell us about that adventure?

LB: Yes, I had created my own brand—Lison Bonfils—and at first it went very well. I had designed the label picturing an elegant woman who loved to be "comfortable," so it was simple but highly manicured. For one summer collection I designed a poplin skirt with a 1.5-centimeter linked silk border. I enjoyed it, we shared a passion, and sure, I sometimes asked my friends to model for me.

↗ Group photograph in Paris, 1970. We can make out Lison Bonfils, Didier Bernardin, Silvia Bocchese, and Giuseppe Bocchese

CB: So, you've worked in both France and in Italy: how would you describe these two, different experiences?

LB: The question implies an answer that has to do with both politics and history. France was a country in which the bourgeoisie had amassed great fortunes, especially in the North, with large industries that made different investments, developing supermarkets, for example. In Italy, on the other hand, there was less wealth, but there was great energy rooted in the territory and a desire to emerge. This happened mainly in Vicenza, which mustn't be confused with the rest of the Veneto region: here the industrial drive has always been quite strong.

CB: You were friends with Azzedine Alaïa, too?

LB: Of course, he was a friend. He was also my daughter Ortensia's godfather. For her fourth birthday she asked him for a fairy costume: Azzedine spent months setting aside pieces of lace, which he then used to make her a magnificent blue dress that Ortensia wore every time the occasion required an elegant attire. For her wedding, he presented her with an extraordinary wedding dress in nylon knitwear, a kind of cellophane that looked like a textile, produced *chez* Miles in Vicenza.

A Legacy of Knitwear

Adam Jones

I first discovered machine knitting at fashion college in the UK in the 1980s. The whole class followed a mandatory workshop for a week, learning to use domestic knitting machines. I had seen machines like these before on the tv, smiley ladies knitting scary looking sweaters and scarves in lurid sparkly yarns.

The prospect was amusing but unappealing to me, I couldn't imagine how this activity could help me achieve my dream of becoming a fashion designer but as I experimented with the machine, I was amazed to see that by playing with the simple techniques that we were taught and mixing the few available yarns, wonderful textures and patterns appeared before me.

I knew right then that I had found my passion, as improbable and unexpected as it was, I knew that I wanted to learn as much as I possibly could about designing knitwear.

A leap forward to 2024 and I am writing this from my office at IFM in Paris where I direct the knitwear programs in the department that I created in 2018.

My students still begin their knitting journey using hand machines very similar to the one I learnt on, but we also have a big park of industrial knitting machines and computers to program the latest software. Knit design has become much more sophisticated but the excitement and joy that it brings to young designers remains unchanged.

Knitwear is fascinating because it is inevitably connected to the production process. Historically, the key designers in the evolution of knitwear have been inextricably linked to the factories that bought their creative visions to life. Many of these designers passed through the now legendary doors of Miles and collaborated with Silvia Bocchese.

Sonia Rykiel reigned through the 70s and 80s as the crowned Queen of knit, her vivid stripes and reverse knit sweaters put knitted silhouettes firmly on the catwalk.

Knitwear through these decades was also dominated by Kenzo with his multi-colored jacquards and Gaultier with his bold patterns and eclectic designs but it was Azzedine Alaïa who opened the door to the future and showed everyone what knitwear could be.

A master of cutting, he understood the human form and draped fabric like a sculptor. His skill, when combined with Silvia Bocchese's technical innovation and the perfect stretch yarn, created for Alaïa by Giuliano Coppini at Linea Piu was the perfect alchemy. A new type of knitwear was created that surpassed everything that had gone before.

Last year I had the pleasure of accompanying my students to visit Miles where we discovered their wonderful archive that lovingly traces the life's work of Silvia Bocchese spanning six decades of creativity, craftsmanship and technical excellence.

It was fascinating to see intricate knitted lace pieces from 80s Valentino, to see the raw creativity of Vivienne Westwood's smock dresses from the 90's, felted and distressed looking as exciting and relevant as the day they were designed. The students loved the retro chic of the Marc Jacob's separates from the 2000s and the graphic motifs and embroideries of recent Bottega Veneta collections.

The cherry on the cake was to see and touch the iconic knits that Miles had developed for Alaïa over the last forty years. The improbable mixes of boiled wool, viscose and raffia in the most incredible knitted techniques, the shapes clean and precise, as if cut by a surgeon's scalpel.

The students were amazed and inspired by the creativity and the technicity of what they saw, they came away even more determined to become knitwear designers and make their own mark on the fashion industry.

Adam Jones

An "A-Typical," "Outmoded" Woman and Entrepreneur

Daniele Marini

I meet Silvia Stein Bocchese in a conference room at Miles.[1] The conversation opens with the illustration of a number of frames hanging on the walls, each dedicated to one of the fashion designers with whom she has worked over the years: Armani, Lagerfeld, Valentino, Chloé, Saint Laurent, Alaïa just to mention a few. Photographs, fabric, sketches, autographed drawings of garments: these are the contents of the frames, eloquently illustrating the relationships she entertained with the greatest international designers.

She describes them with passion and engagement, while at the same time making her personality manifest, her manner of conducting both her relations and her business, her vision of life, which is intertwined with her entrepreneurial identity. Her values are rooted in a universe defined by the intersection of Jewish and Protestant culture, inspired by devotion to work, independence, industriousness, but also the ability to delegate and thus empower others, whether they are her children or her collaborators: being at the heart of the enterprise without centralizing.

The aspect of gender, her being a mother and a female entrepreneur, didn't have a particular characterization to her eyes or in her life, she did not perceive a divide with her male colleagues. This is the mark of a pragmatic way of thinking and living, where equality is in objects and in relations: a given fact.

Her dedication to her undertaking and to her entrepreneurial vision, sometimes forgoing easier and more immediate profits, is the philosophy that places this company in an area of the market with a very high added value and renders it unique in its field. All of this, adopting the "nudge"[2] style or, as her son Michele puts it, with a "determined composure," an aspect that becomes obvious during our conversation by her habit of always looking her interlocutor in the eye.

We may well say, with a play on words, that Silvia Bocchese is an "outmoded" woman and entrepreneur—in the statistical sense: where "mode" is the most common value that ap-

pears in a set universe, she places herself decidedly "outside the box," with her uniqueness and distinctiveness, both on a personal and on an entrepreneurial level.

The experiences of Silvia Bocchese, woman and entrepreneur, bear similarities and dif-
ferences with many of the entrepreneurial stories typical of the development of Veneto
and the Northeast before it became the "engine of the country," as it has been called.
But let us proceed in order and consider some of the most noteworthy aspects of her
"a-typicality."

Silvia Bocchese came to Italy, to Schio, from Switzerland right after the war (1948). These
were the years of the post-war reconstruction, and Veneto was a territory marked by a
strong agricultural vocation and a "rural" culture, while its manufacturing activities were
mainly represented by very small, artisanal activities. In national iconography, Northeast
Italy, which was called Triveneto at the time, was considered the "South in the North":
an economically depressed area, where the birthrate was much higher than the national
average and poverty was still very widespread. Just think of the Italian movies produced
at the time: the waiters and the soldiers were always played by actors with a Venetian or
Friulan accent.

Politically speaking, in the 1948 elections the Christian Democracy collected 60% of the
votes in Veneto, which rose to 71.9% in the province of Vincenza. This was the era of
"single color" local administrations and the Christian Democracy dominated the political
scenario. It is not by chance that on a national level these areas were known as "Vandee
bianche," white zones, because of the nearly unanimous backing of the party of Christian inspiration.

The Catholic church was widespread and deeply rooted in this territory, to the point that it was considered a "from the bottom up" welfare system: parish centers, cinemas, theaters, athletic fields, spaces where associations could meet. To this day, the pre-school and nursery school system are a prevalently Catholic domain. At the time, more or less 80% of the population attended mass. Furthermore, a very structured system of associations gravitated around the Church and were inspired by its precepts: Azione Cattolica (AC, Catholic Action), the Associazioni Cristiane dei lavoratori italiani (ACLI, the Christian Associations of Italian Workers), and the Scout Movement. On the labor front, the Confederazione italiana sindacati lavoratori (CISL, Italian Confederation of Worker Unions) led the way. Research carried out on the first ACLI[3] associations showed that members of this group were often members of CISL and Democrazia Cristiana, too. Much the same happened on the opposing front, in the "red" areas of the country, where cardholders of the Italian Communist Party were most often members of the Confederazione generale italiana del lavoro (CGIL, General Italian Confederation of Workers) as well as of the Associazione ricreativa e culturale italiana (ARCI, Italian Cultural and Recreational Association). Each of these was a strictly defined, homogenous universe with their symbols and values mostly overlapping.

In Veneto, Catholic moral and political belonging were basic paradigms for the construction of the society and economy of the time.

Silvia Bocchese was the bearer of a different, "a-typical" experience. Her roots lay in another, different context:

> My father Theodor, whose parents were Jewish, was never a religiously observant man. The youngest of six siblings, he held a degree in engineering, had worked with Einstein, and was a member of the New York Academy of Sciences. He designed electric turbines, and so was made director of De Pretto-Escher Wyss in Schio. For this reason, we moved to Italy in 1948. My mother, on the other hand, was Protestant. My father was her second husband, and she was my father's third wife.

We can imagine that coming to a smaller reality such as Schio, a fundamentally mono-cultural environment, could trigger a sort of "cognitive shock," or a process of passive adaptation and compliance. But this did not happen. In her stories we find, instead, an affirmation of her social and cultural identity that for her parents implied behaviors that they had no fear in putting into practice even though they were considered unorthodox.

> When they moved to Schio, she [my mother] went out every evening with her friends. They played cards, poker—she was very good. Then they went dancing, they went out to dinner, while my father only took Saturday nights off. They both had an attitude towards workers that was different for the times. Mother organized parties for the employees, she gave their children gifts, and she played bocce and danced with them. My father created the Circolo ricreativo aziendale dei lavoratori (CRAL, Company Workers' Recreational Club), which had a cafeteria, a bocce field, and rooms where small parties could be held. He was much loved by his employees, though at first they had been a little suspicious, accustomed as their were to a strict distinction of roles.

Within this experience lies Silvia Bocchese's universe of reference and a first mark of "a-typicality": she grew up in a culturally open environment that did not fear to exhibit and act upon its own criteria, escaping a petit-bourgeois rhetoric and a need to conform to the mores and customs of the time. And this translated into a choice of clothing, a juvenile whim, as she says she was: "one of the first people to wear jeans, which my father had brought from New York."

These are the terms in which she expresses her values of independence and responsibility, the pivots of her parenting experience, echoes of which may be found in her approach to business:

> I tried to be [with my children] at important times, without obsessing over them. As had been done for me, I gave them plenty of freedom and trust; I always tried to let them act autonomously. Then I told them: "Should you decide to join the business some day, I'll be very happy, but each of you should do as they feel."

A second mark of her "a-typicality" may be observed in her entrepreneurial experience. She started her business together with a few other people in 1962. She already had two children, but she couldn't see herself following the path taken by most women her age at that time: taking on the exclusive role of mother and housewife. Her complicity with her husband was such that she decided to start her own business, although his family seemed perplexed by this choice and despite the stereotypes that would have tied her to a role in which she did not see herself: "Even when I got married, I was always free. My husband made this possible, for he understood that I didn't see myself as a homemaker. [...] And my mother was a huge help."

Once again, what emerges is the strength of subjective identity, of imagining oneself taking paths that don't follow a tradition or roles prefigured by the social and cultural context of the time. However, all this happened *in medias res*, as a part of things, in the peaceful course of her personal experiences: she enacted a sort of "quiet revolution." Despite the historical setting of her story (the years of the cultural upheavals of students and workers between the 1960s and 1970s), her narrative doesn't contain vindicative elements. There is no trace of what we might call a feminist orientation. Everything happened naturally, without considering or underlining a difference in gender. Even when it came to her entrepreneurial experience.

A third "a-typical" aspect consequently lies in the management of her business. Where the prevailing conception in the collective imagery was that of the "master," the solitary leader of a company where workers were subordinates when not downright exploited, for Silvia Bocchese it was just the opposite. Her style in guiding and managing the company closely resembled the way she raised her children, in the name of facts as opposed to words. "I am of few words, but everyday life has some rules: respect for people, devotion to work, passion for what you do, seriousness, and the ability to govern certain situations."

A "gentle nudge" before it became "a thing," before behavioral studies grasped and defined this mode of management. A shared leadership that she attempted to spread to other colleagues in this industry, though to little or no avail:

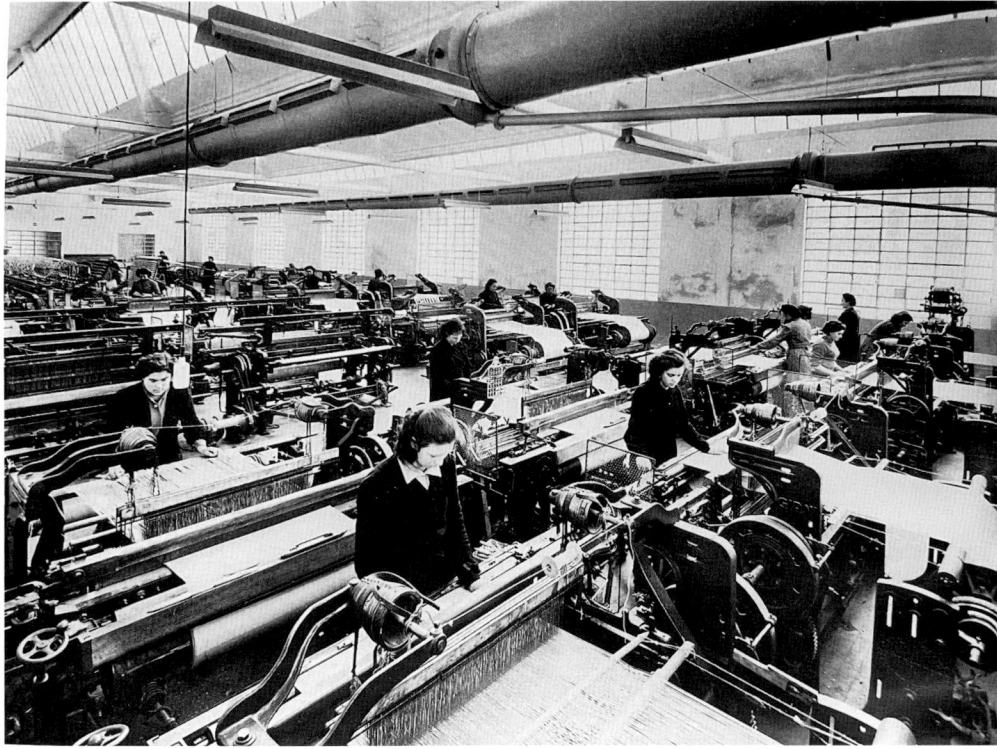

One difficulty I encountered was in creating synergies with other companies: when the business was growing in the 1970s and 1980s, becoming an important player in the sector, I tried to involve my colleagues, because I have always believed that cooperation is important. However, I often came up against the strong individualism of other entrepreneurs, which left little space for productive collaboration.

Silvia Bocchese was faced with the cultural inclination most typical of Northeastern entrepreneurs: each was king of one's own castle, and neighbors were seen more as rivals than potential associates.

These were the years of the economic growth of what would soon come to be known as the Northeast, or the "engine of the country," thanks to its financial prowess, its GDP growing at a 5% yearly rate, much like what is happening today in countries such as China and India. This was the epic of the birth and formation of the industrial districts, triggered by the crisis of the large Fordist industries and a process of deindustrialization that pushed many skilled workers to open their own businesses and become entrepreneurs. "Small is Beautiful"[4] takes its revenge on the Fordist behemoths. Scholars such as Giorgio Fuà and Carlo Zacchia,[5] or Arnaldo Bagnasco[6] considered the so-called "Third Italy" and the Northeast-Center—scattered with small and medium businesses—an area capable of growing and producing wealth, though economic theories said the opposite. The pride of many a worker turned small entrepreneur, who by toiling tirelessly produced an unprecedented growth, also nurtured a tendency to be independent, individualistic, and have a heightened sense of ownership, which didn't leave much room for the idea of cooperating with others. In this context, Silvia Bocchese's approach was once again "a-typical," going against the grain, albeit frustrated by the lack of sensitivity and sharing shown by her colleagues.

However, her entrepreneurial endeavor also contains an element of "typicality," of kinship with the spirit of the Northeast: the concept of work as an ideal. The Northeast is surely a supporter of "Labor,"[7] though not in a political sense, but rather because it finds

↗ Giuseppe Bocchese & Figli silk factory, interiors of the Vicenza plant, circa 1960

Daniele Marini

44

in Labor (with a capital L) an element of identity and social cohesion. Everyone identified (and for the most part still identifies) with work as "society in action." In the past century, during the years of economic growth, most people worked and many held more than one job at the same time: a prime example of this being the figure of the "metalmezzadro,"[8] a metalworker (*metalmeccanico*) who worked a factory shift by day and went to work the fields (*mezzadro* = sharecropper) when the shift ended. Their drive was the desire to leave poverty behind and access a condition of greater stability and wealth, the trigger of a social elevation activated by getting things done without expecting help.

Silvia Bocchese's approach fed on a culture that was both Jewish and Protestant, and fit in perfectly with the local mores.

> For a while I worked with my father at his office. I was his secretary, I archived his documents, which is something I really enjoy. After spending some time in London and Lausanne perfecting my language skills, I took a course in mathematics, where I also learned shorthand and other such things, and then I went back to work with my father until I got married.

She never backed down, even when faced with the difficulties she later encountered (the death of her husband in 1973, the fire at the plant in 1980). In fact, these urged her on, always on her own:

> The first great challenge was when my husband died in a car crash in 1973. After that, my brother-in-law Rino offered to take over the commercial management of the silk factory, which was my husband's job. I thought it over and then said no. At that point Miles was growing steadily and I told myself that I wanted to try to carry on on my own. [...] And then the terrible fire in 1980.

Work and independence are two distinctive features of Silvia Bocchese's character, a common trait of both her entrepreneurial daring and the spirit of the Northeast. In this sense, we can see a kinship between the person and the territory that adopted her, albeit expressed through an experience that was decidedly "a-typical" for the context in which it flourished. If we think of the sector in which she operated, we might say that it was both "tailor made" and "outmoded."

1   This piece is based on a conversation with Silvia Stein Bocchese and her son Michele Bocchese at the Miles offices in Vicenza on March 20, 2024. The dialog was led by Daniele Marini and Irene Lovato Menin. Daniele Marini is responsible for this text, using parts of the conversation as elaborated by Irene Lovato Menin.

2   See Thaler and Sunstein 2008.
3   Marini 1987.
4   Schumacher 1973.
5   Fuà and Zacchia 1983.
6   Bagnasco 1977.
7   Marini 2015.
8   Bernardi 1987.

MILES

album

"As for the textile for the silk collar, I had a wealth of choice."

Silvia Bocchese

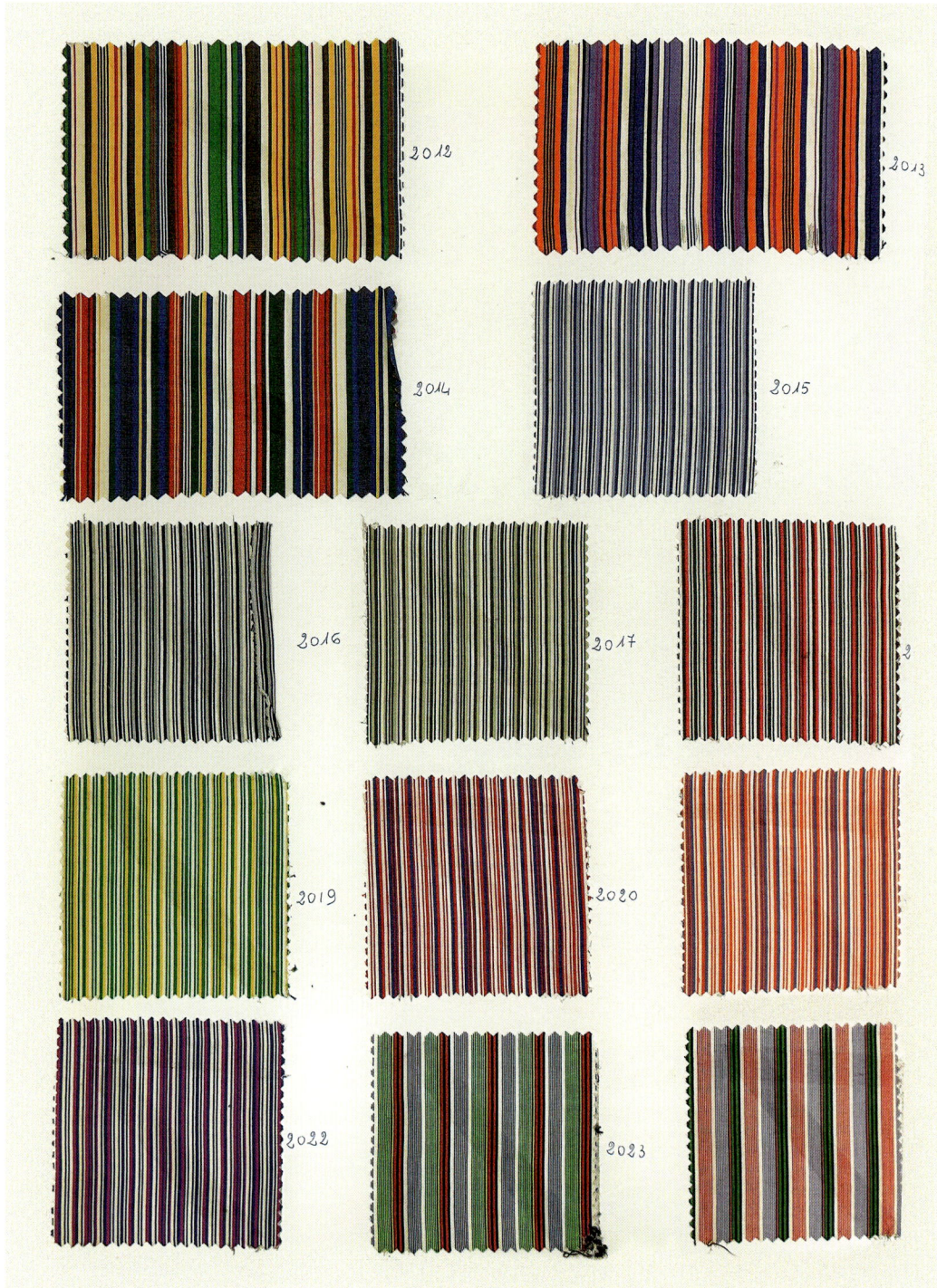

Samples of Liberty silks produced
by Giuseppe Bocchese & Figli

Miles shantung polo shirt with Liberty silk applique by Giuseppe Bocchese & Figli, 1968–1969

"In 1970, I decided to buy my cashmere from Todd & Duncan; they replied with a letter saying that before they could sell to me, they would have to visit the company to verify our yarn-treatment procedures. When they got to Vicenza, they had no doubts, and I began producing Scottish cashmere sweaters."

Silvia Bocchese

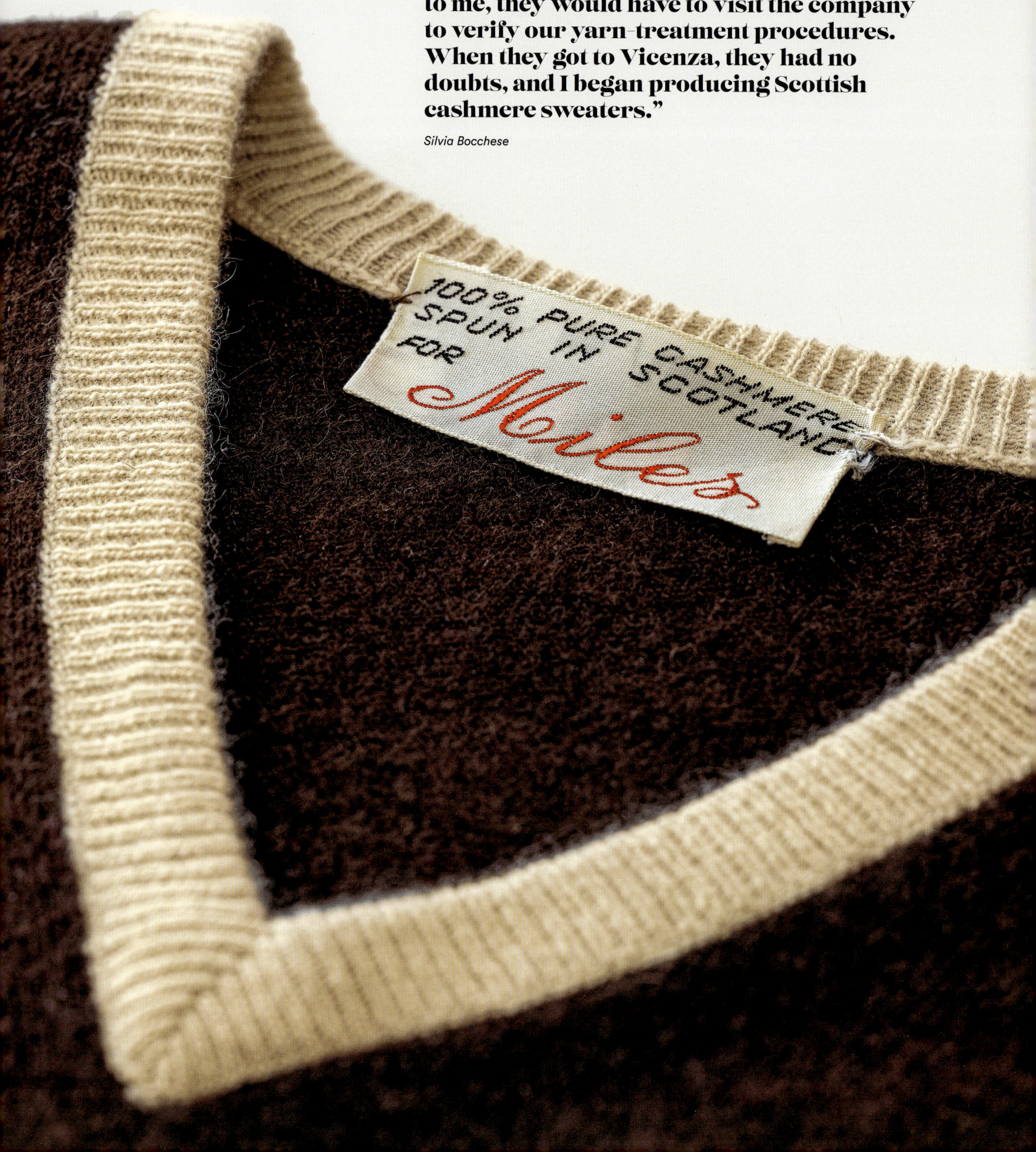

100% PURE CASHMERE
SPUN IN SCOTLAND
FOR
Miles

Tableau composed by Silvia Bocchese
with mementos from her collaboration
with Yves Saint Laurent

Lurex vest developed for Yves Saint Laurent,
1973 summer collection

E 74

B.278

VESTE BICOLORE

série 167

01 - marine - blanc

03 - carmin - blanc

05 - emeraude - blanc

SAINT LAURENT
rive gauche

Two-tone wool jacket developed for Saint Laurent
Rive Gauche, 1974 summer collection

Wool sweater with detachable collar
developed for Chloé, 1974 winter collection

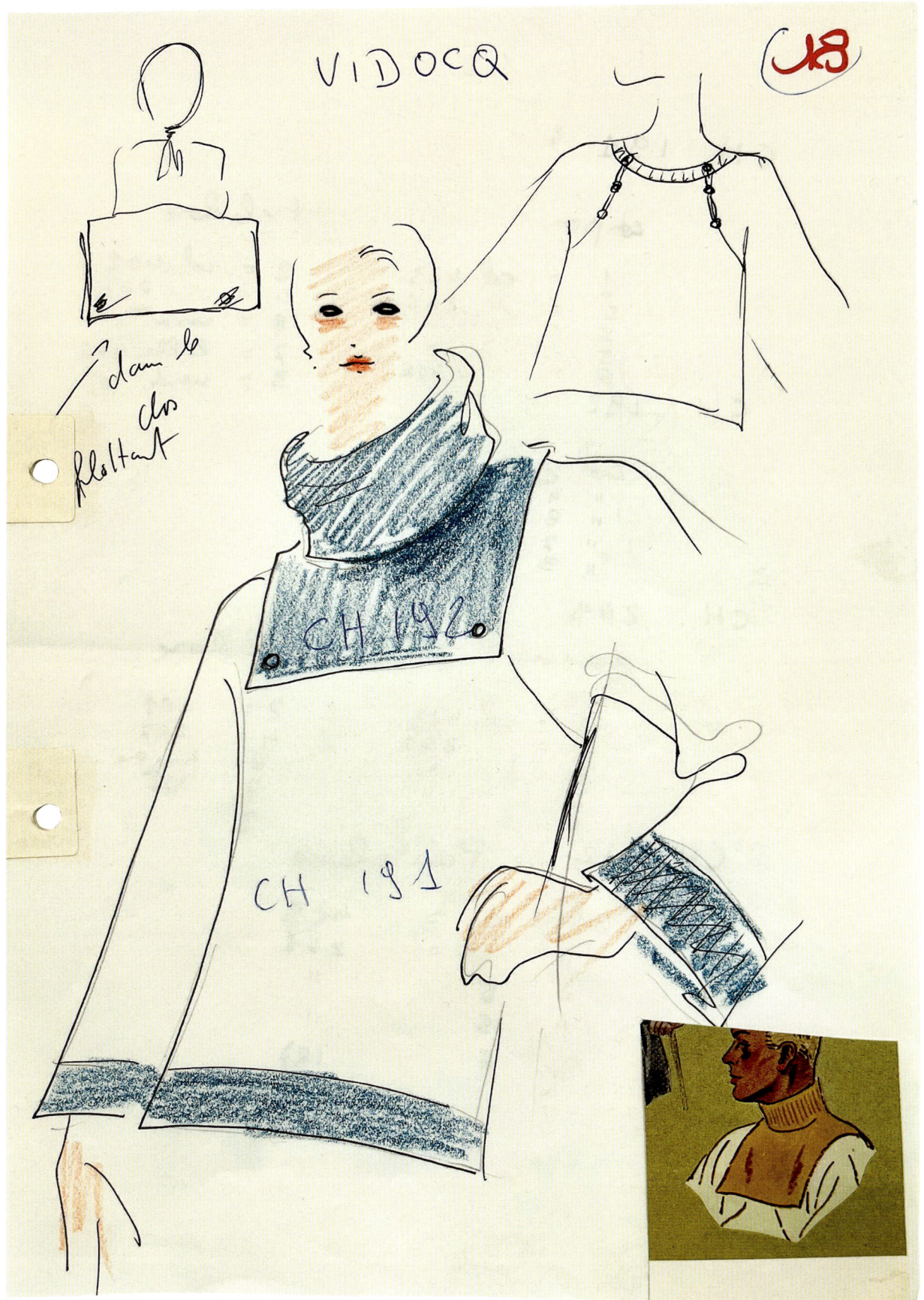

Karl Lagerfeld, sketch for Chloé turtleneck
sweater, 1974, pen and colored pencil, 40 × 30 cm

Miles

Lurex vest developed for Yves Saint Laurent, 1975
summer collection

Sketch by the *maison* Yves Saint Laurent,
pencil on paper, notes in pen, 30 × 21 cm, 1975

Embroidered wool sweater developed
for Yves Saint Laurent, 1977 summer collection

Sketch by the *maison* Yves Saint Laurent,
pencil and colored pencil on paper, 30 × 21 cm,
1977

Swatches for color variants for the Yves
Saint Laurent cotton pullover displayed
on the next page

Maison Miles.

Série 15

61

63

62

64

65

Cotton pullover developed for Yves Saint Laurent,
1977 summer collection

Tableau composed by Silvia Bocchese
with mementos from her collaboration
with Chloé

Fur-stich cotton bolero developed for Chloé,
1979 summer collection

Karl Lagerfeld, sketch for a fur stitch Chloé
pullover, pen, marker, colored pencil and collage,
40 × 30 cm, 1979

Album

VOTRE MAILLOT APRÈS LE COUCHER DU SOLEIL

Superbe maillot nageur en fil à fil, en échancré haut sur les cuisses, en version piscine et en version après-bain, avec une ceinture en raphia et cuir, gants assortis. (Le tout : Alaïa, 465 F le maillot). Boucles d'oreilles (Marie Beltrami).

Joli coup de filet

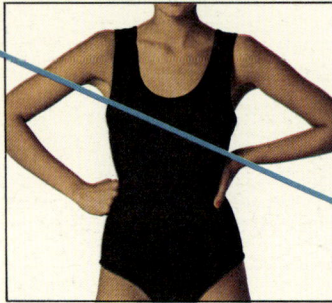

Duc

Alaïa belt and bodysuit, *Elle* France,
issue #1907, July 26, 1982

Cotton bodysuit for a twine and leather belt
by Alaïa, 1981

Miles

Chloé outfit salvaged from the flames in 1980
and published in the program for the summer 1981
fashion show

063 BATH
72.700

Bustier

gama body 062
68.500

Lison Bonfils, sketch for a bodysuit and a skirt
with frills, marker on paper, 30 × 40 cm, 1981

Album

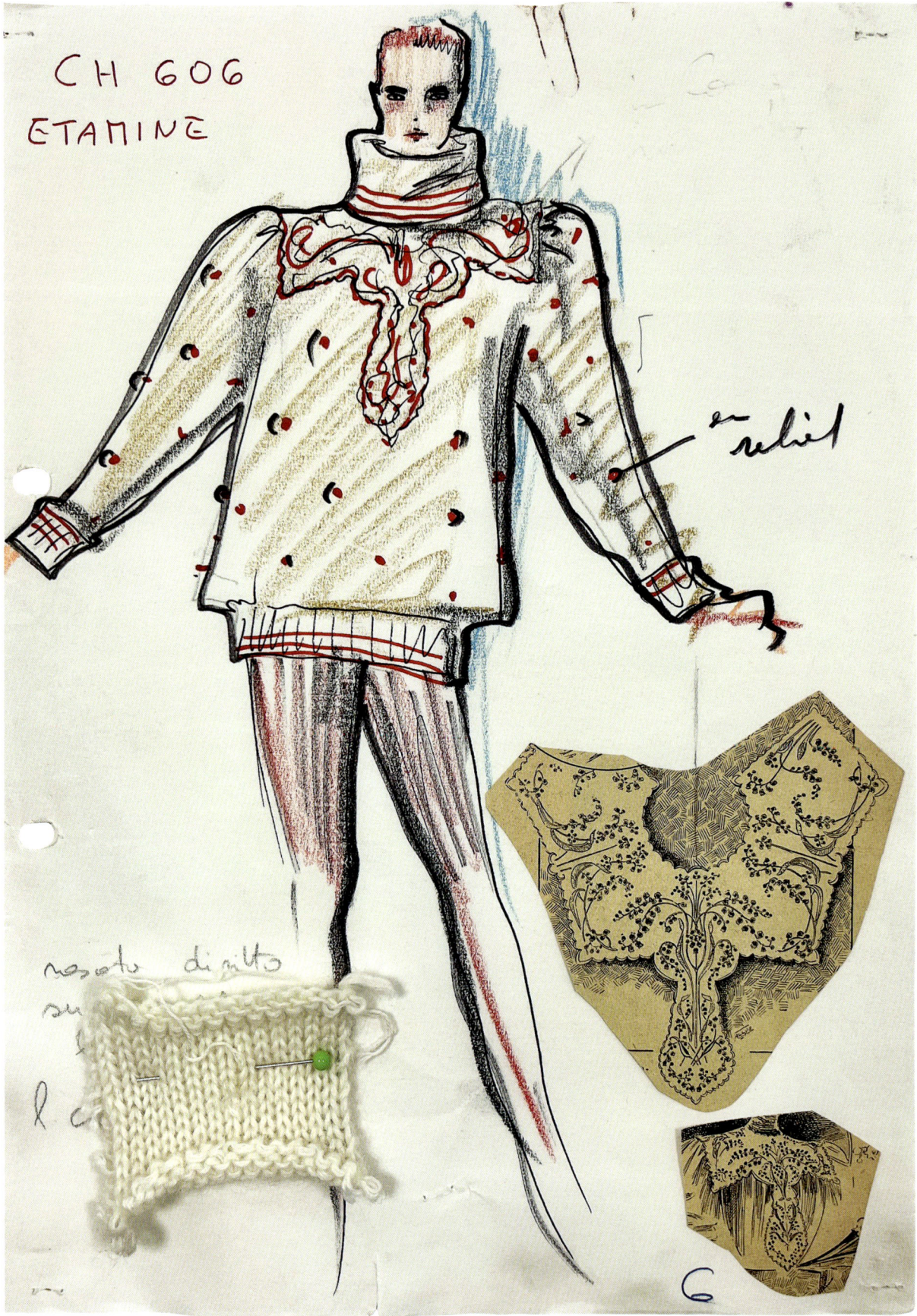

CH 606
ETAMINE

Karl Lagerfeld, sketch for a turtleneck sweater
by Chloé, 1981, pen, marker, colored pencil
and collage, 40 × 30 cm

Les réactions des journalistes new-yorkais. NANCY NEWHOUSE DU « NEW YORK TIMES » : « L'opinion américaine est partagée, l'une trouve cette mode sexiste, l'autre applaudit la beauté et l'allure. » Ici, deux pulls de laine boutonnés sur l'épaule. Gants de cuir rivetés.

Editorial, *Elle* France, issue # 1921,
November 1, 1982

CINIGLIA

M.108
c. nero.

H116
c. grigio
+ oro

M103
c. nero.

M104

c. nero

M106
c. nero

M109
c. nero
c. grigio
+ oro

M105
c. nero

M101
c. nero

M102
c. nero

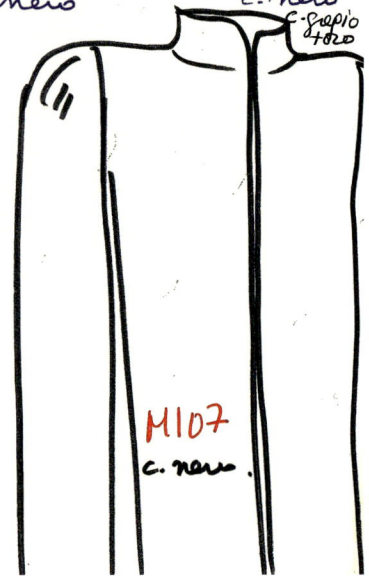

M107
c. nero.

Lison Bonfils, sketches for chenille garments,
marker and pen on paper, 40 × 30 cm, 1982

Chenille outfit developed for Lison Bonfils,
1982 winter collection

Silvia Bocchese in front of the Céline boutique
in Miami, late 1970s

Wool sweater with leather bands
and metal buttons developed for Céline,
1984 winter collection

Sketch for a piece from Alaïa's summer
1985 collection, pencil on paper and collage,
30 × 21 cm

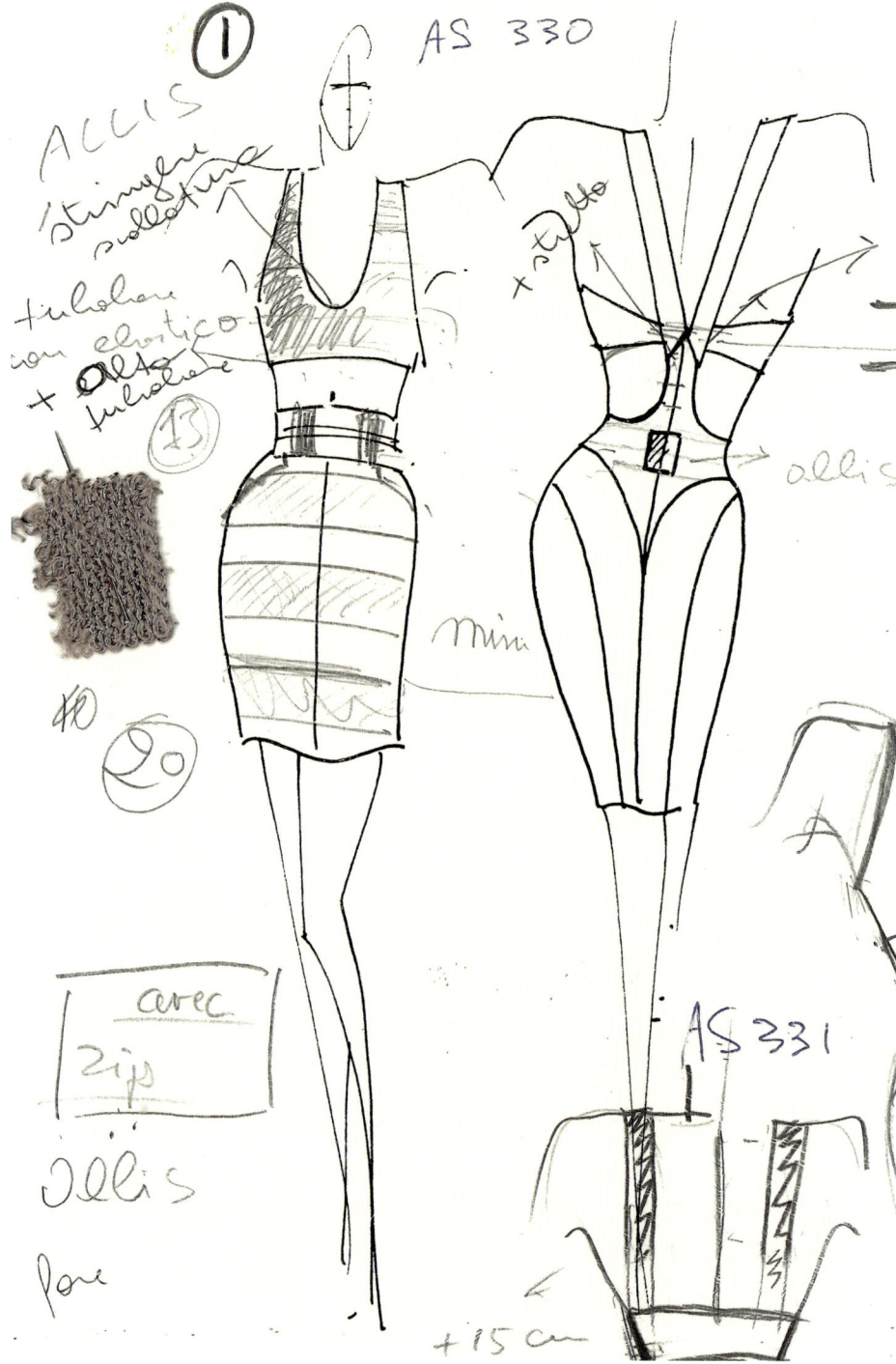

Viscose dress developed for Alaïa,
1985 summer collection

ALAIA : LA MAILLE EN SUPER VEDETTE

Azzedine Alaïa : le roi de la maille unie, perfectionne-t-il au maximum cet hiver Son concept? Confort ultra de la matière; précision astucieuse de la coupe; formes les plus simples qui mettent le corps à l'aise et en valeur « Un pull, un fuseau, un body, une jupe, un collant les bases importantes. Importantes aussi : la censure, pour l'aplomb, la taille, et les chaussures plates ou à talon, pour la jambe, la silhouette. » Typée, la mode d'Alaïa se suffit à elle-même. Pas de bijoux. Une beauté de jour naturelle. « visage lavé, peau soignée, yeux un peu faits, cheveux propres » La femme habillée par Alaïa! Moderne, féminissime, sa personnalité toujours privilégiée, bien dans ses vêtements. « C'est bon pour le moral, ça dope. » Des femmes symboles? Plein, liste enthousiaste, de Paloma Picasso à Tina Turner, d'Arletty à Garbo. Facile de faire simple? « Faire un vêtement très simple et qui tienne debout est le plus difficile » Changer? « L'obsession du neuf-neuf, non! Il faut être fidèle à son esprit, prendre le temps de mûrir » Ci-contre, la leçon de mode d'Azzedine Alaïa quatre porters pour deux pulls en alpaga côtelé et feutré, col montant, beau volume. **1.** Pull court blanc écru, sur fuseau maille jersey. **2.** Pull long vert, sur mini-jupe et collant assortis. **3.** Pull court chocolat, sur pantalon droit gabardine de laine noire. **4.** Pull court framboise, sur jupe juste au-dessus du genou, maille jersey. Accessoires Alaïa Coiffures Carmel pour Saint-Gilles International. Maquillages Christelle pour Faces.

Monographic supplement dedicated to Azzedine Alaïa, *Marie Claire Bis*, Edition speciale mode, October 1985

Wool dress with inlaid wraparound zipper
developed for Alaïa, 1986 winter collection

Viscose dress developed for Alaïa,
1990 summer collection

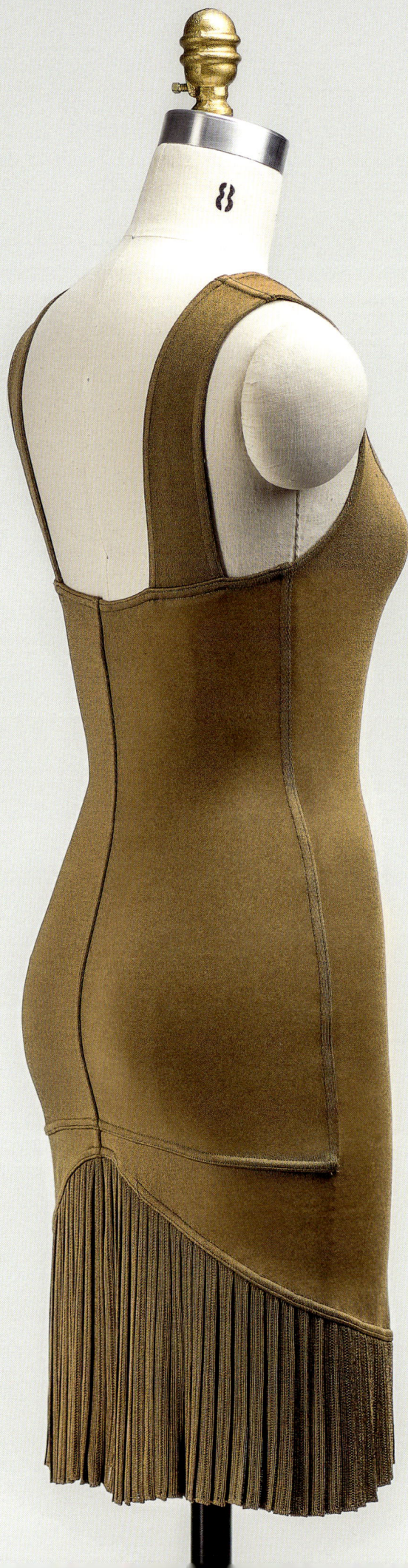

Gilles Bensimon, photo of Alaïa's summer 1990
collection

"I remember I called Alaïa and told him: 'I like your idea of using twine... I like it a bit less when it breaks all the needles in my machines! Never again, Azzedine!'"

Silvia Bocchese

Skirt with *a jour* motif and fur stitch hem
developed for Alaïa, 1991 winter collection

Col
TEDDY

2675

Sketch for a dress with *ajour* motif by Alaïa, 1993
(sales catalog copy)

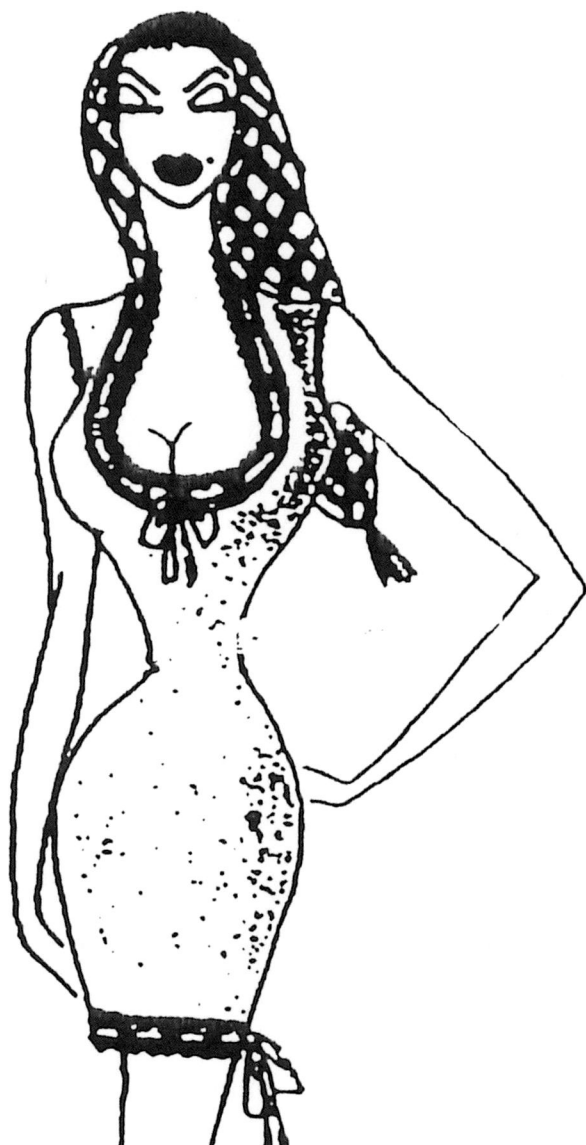

Viscose dress with *a jour* motif
developed for Alaïa, 1993 summer collection

Two Alaïa garments exhibited during the show
at Palazzo Corsini in Florence, 1996

Chenille-effect viscose dress developed for Alaïa, 1993 winter collection

Felted wool lace jacket developed for Alaïa,
1993 winter collection

"The felted wool pieces were born from a series of errors and numerous trials: I remember very well when one of my team—what's more, in front of Alaïa—took the material for a wool coat out of the washing machine and it was barely enough for a jacket. And yet we gradually began producing garments in masterfully felted wool."

Silvia Bocchese

Sketch for an Alaïa jacket, 1993
(sales catalog copy)

Sketch for an Alaïa dress with a stitch sample
attached, 1996 (technical production copy)

Cellophane-effect viscose dress
developed for Alaïa, 1996 summer collection

Cotton bobbin lace dress
developed for Ernestina Cerini,
1995 summer collection

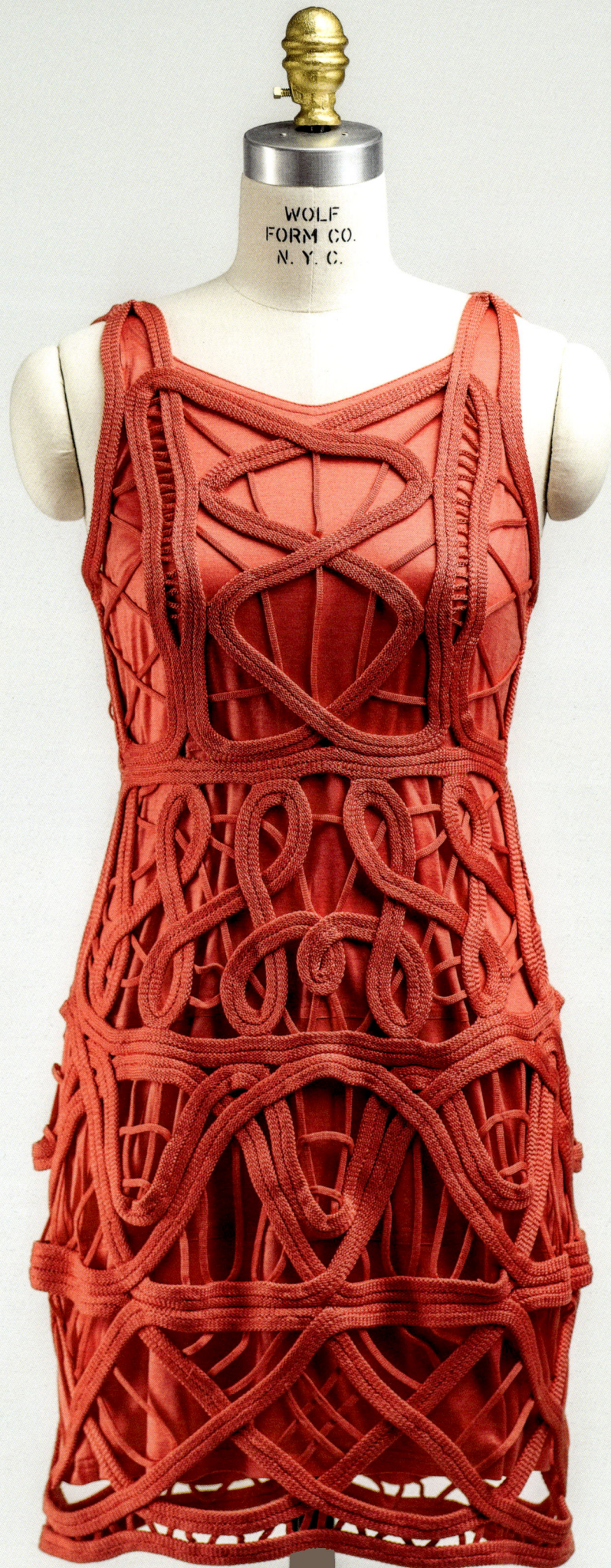

Wool bobbin lace cardigan
developed for Ernestina Cerini,
1996 winter collection

Wool blend embossed jacquard sweater
developed for Ernestina Cerini,
1996 winter collection

Intarsia wool sweater developed for Sonia Rykiel,
1999 winter collection

↙ Intarsia cotton demi-pull skirt with appliqued rhinestones developed for Sonia Rykiel, 1999 winter collection

↘ Intarsia wool skirt developed for Sonia Rykiel, 2002 summer collection

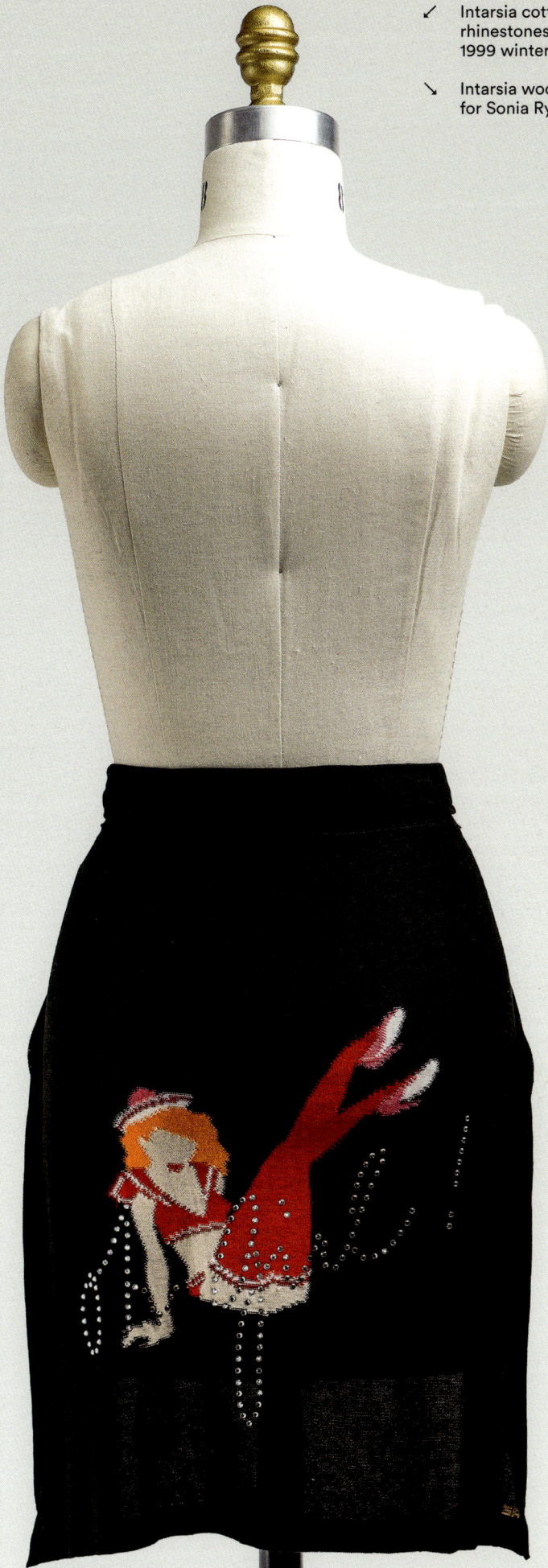

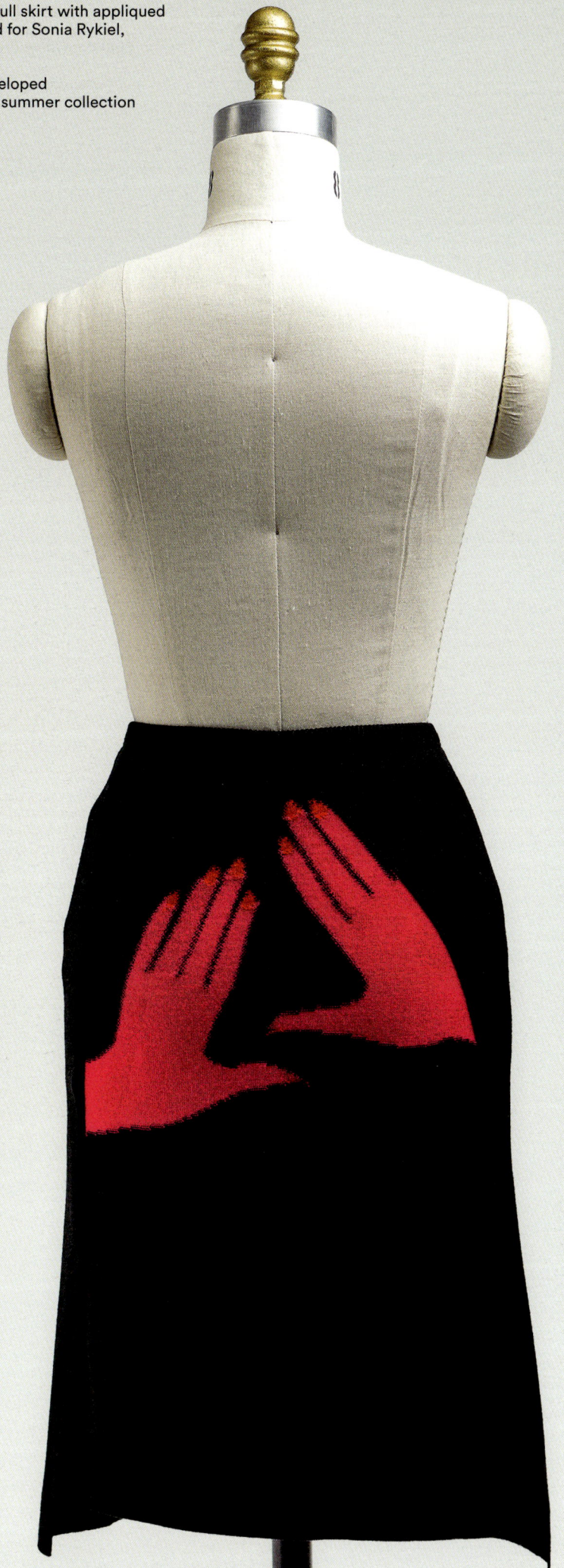

Album

Wool outfit with sequined crochet stars
joined by leather elements, developed for Nude,
2000 winter collection

Mohair sweater with sequins and fur band
developed for Nude, 2000 winter collection

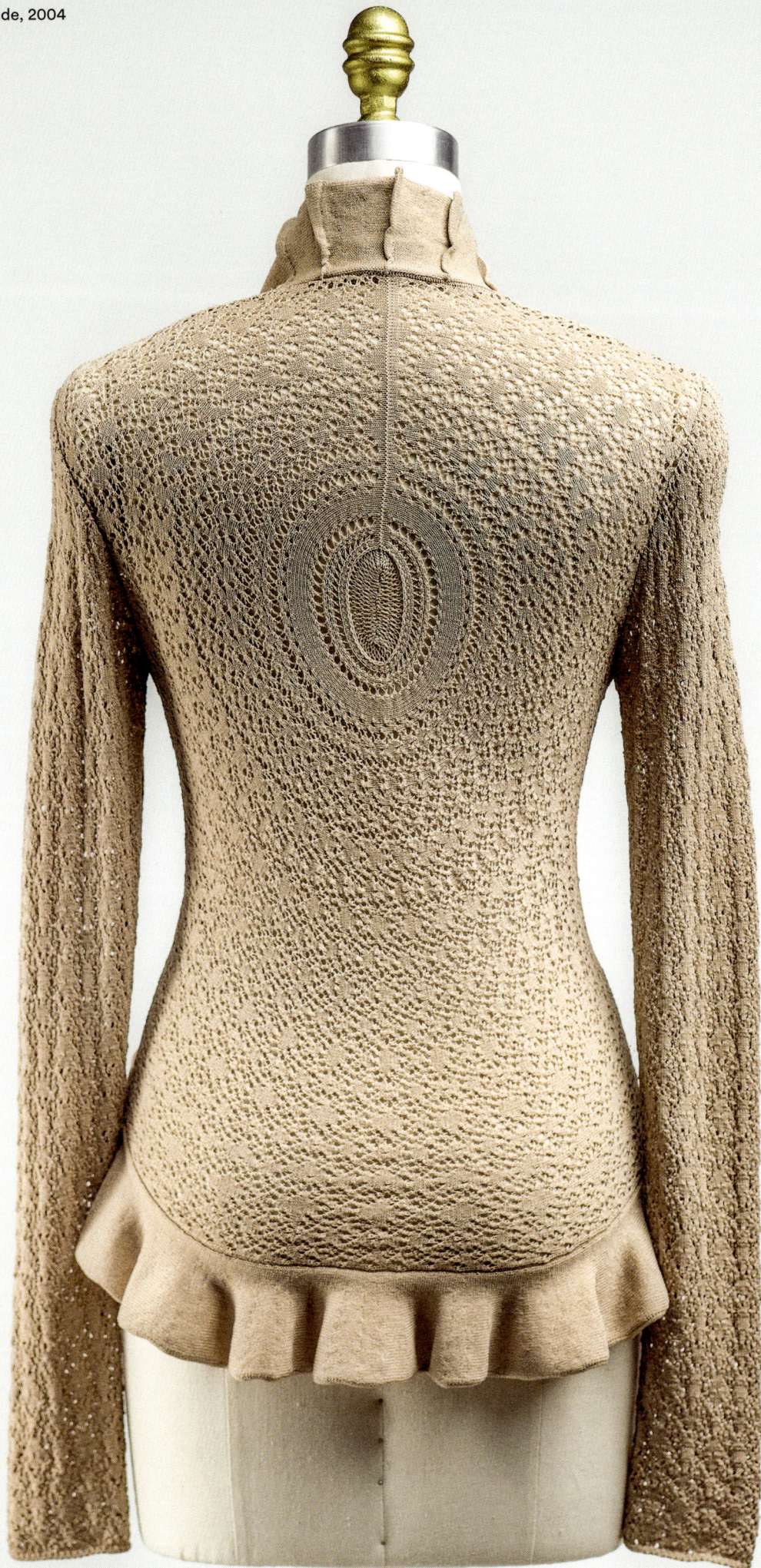

Chenille fur stitched coat developed
for Giorgio Armani, 2003 winter collection

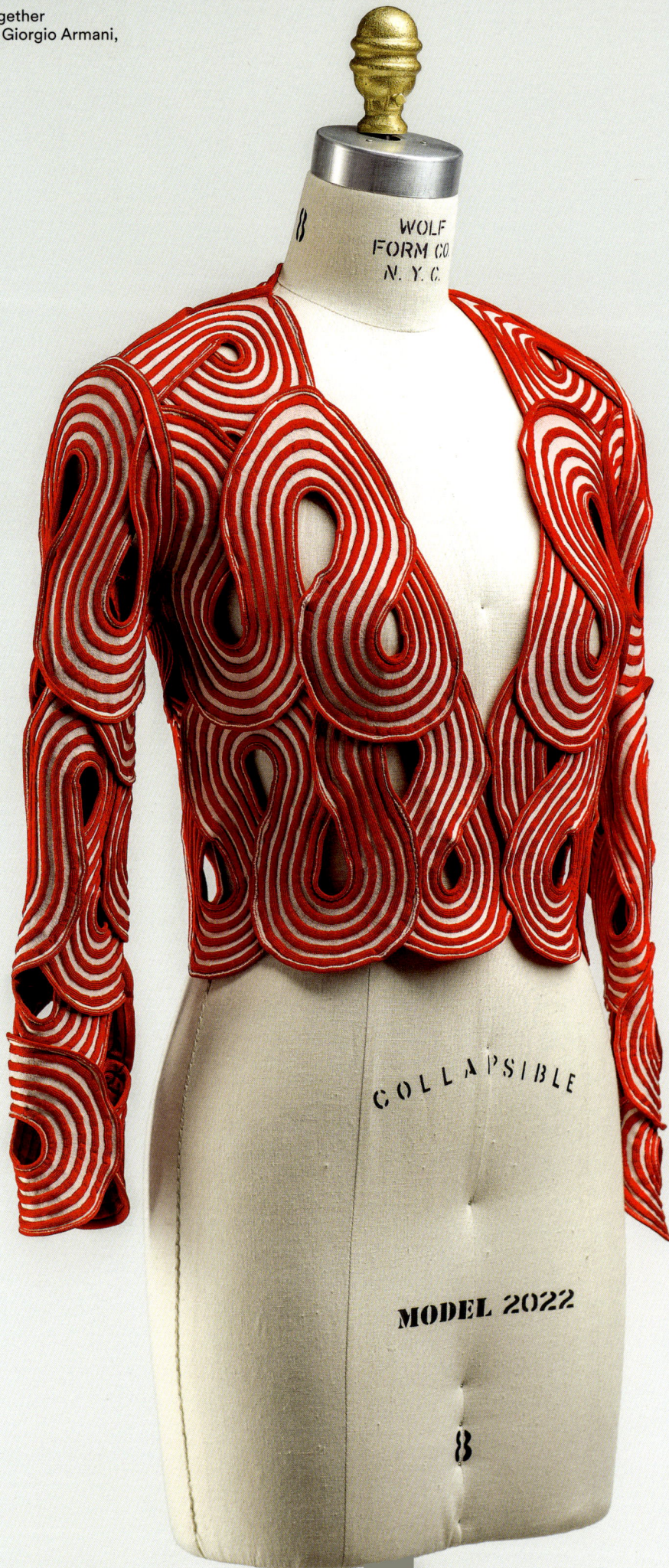

Viscose jacket entirely pieced together
on the mannequin developed for Giorgio Armani,
2004 spring collection

Metallic yarn and silk-cashmere blend jacket
with appliqued viscose mesh developed
for Giorgio Armani, 2005 spring collection

Marc Jacobs

Martedi 18

reference for group 12

* I am trying to get this exact yarn sent to you.

Marc loves this!

thank - you.

Jacket knit using the same wool yarn used for the woven fabric with velvet collar developed for Marc Jacobs, 2005 winter collection

Skirt created by Orsola de Castro
with pieces of cloth leftover
from other brands, year 2005

"When I showed up at Miles for the first time
in 2001, the idea of sustainable fashion didn't yet
exist [...] I began picking scraps off the floor,
the workers looking at me as if I were nuts!
I gradually began to compose a garment on myself,
placing everything I found on the ground onto my
own body. The forewoman immediately got what
I was doing and together we hurried to salvage
entire bags of scraps.
With Silvia Bocchese's consent, of course.
She understood my creative process as well
as my dedication to the environment—she was
ahead of her time.
That adventure ended in 2024, and aside from
a number of garments, I still have a box in my
studio with some 'treats' I took home from that
experience: laces, buttons and appliques that
Silvia set aside for me."

Orsola de Castro, founder of From Somewhere and author of *Loved Clothes Last*
(London: Penguin, 2021)

Striped cotton jacket developed for Sonia Rykiel,
2006 summer collection

Tableau composed by Silvia Bocchese
with mementos from her collaboration
with Sonia Rykiel

Cotton dress with several lace
and crinoline bands developed for Alaïa,
2007 summer collection

Viscose skirt with alternating lace and frills
developed for Alaïa, 2008 summer collection

Album

Viscose dress developed for Alaïa,
2008 summer collection

Miles

Miles

"Until I met Silvia Bocchese in 2009, I had always made my garments by hand, inventing the pieces as I went along. Entrusting technicians and machines with my story was a huge step for me, but from our very first meeting nothing seemed impossible any longer. I had no doubt Silvia shared my passion for knitwear, or more precisely for the art of knitting, and that her knowledge in this field was unique. My knit garments imply creative freedom. I always base my creations on the human body, I am fascinated by the way a garment can enhance, distort or transform a silhouette. In this sense, my creative approach is more similar to that of a sculptor than of a tailor."

Sandra Backlund

Wool tunic developed for Sandra Backlund,
2010 summer collection

Wool and viscose dress developed for Alaïa,
2010 winter collection

Miles

WOLF
FORM CO.
N. Y. C.

154

Silk dress with ruffles developed for Alaïa,
2011 spring collection

Metallic thread skirt with silk ruffles
and colored viscose bands developed for Alaïa,
2011 summer collection

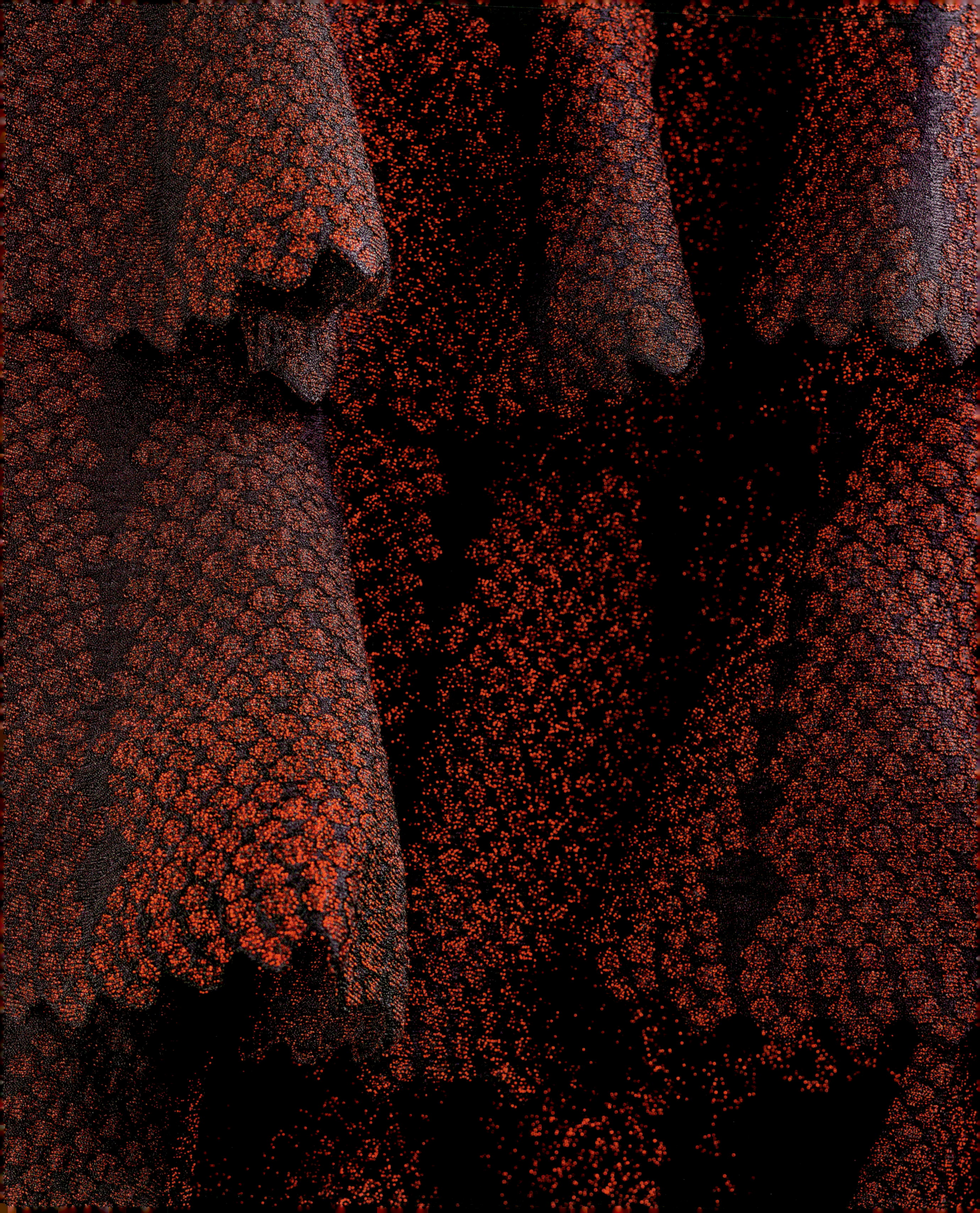

Viscose and lurex thread dress
developed for Alaïa, winter couture
fashion show 2011

Viscose *animalier* jacquard velvet dress
developed for Alaïa, 2011 winter collection

Miles

Velvet dress with lace inlay developed for Alaïa,
2014 winter collection

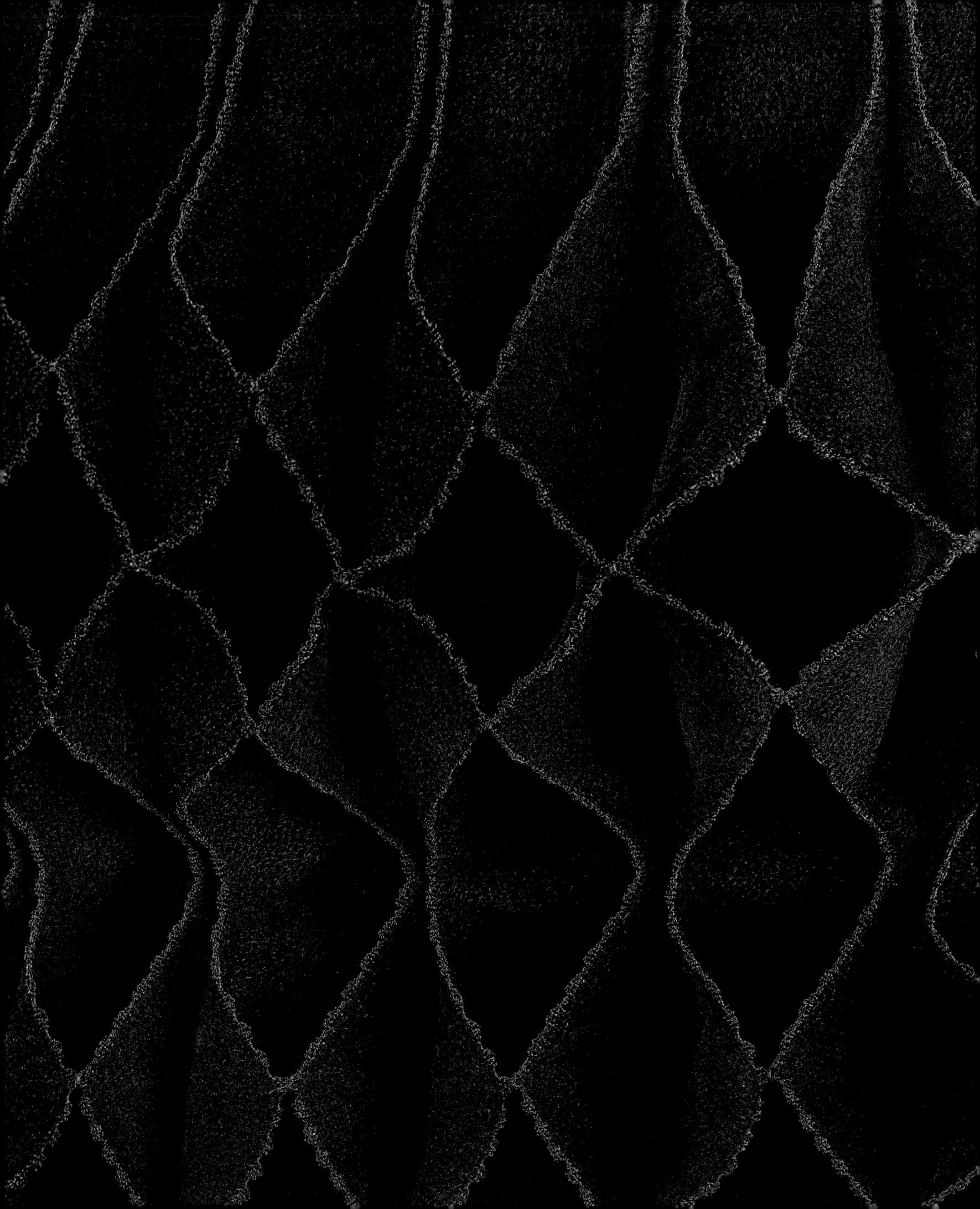

Miles

Silk and raffia dress developed for Alaïa,
2016 summer collection

Cotton blend dress with color-gradient frills
developed for Sonia Rykiel, 2016 summer
collection

Jacquard viscose dress with appliqued studs
developed for Alaïa, 2016 winter collection

Wool and viscose dress with 3D effect motif
developed for Alaïa, 2016 winter collection

On the runway at Alaïa's couture fashion
show in Paris, 2017

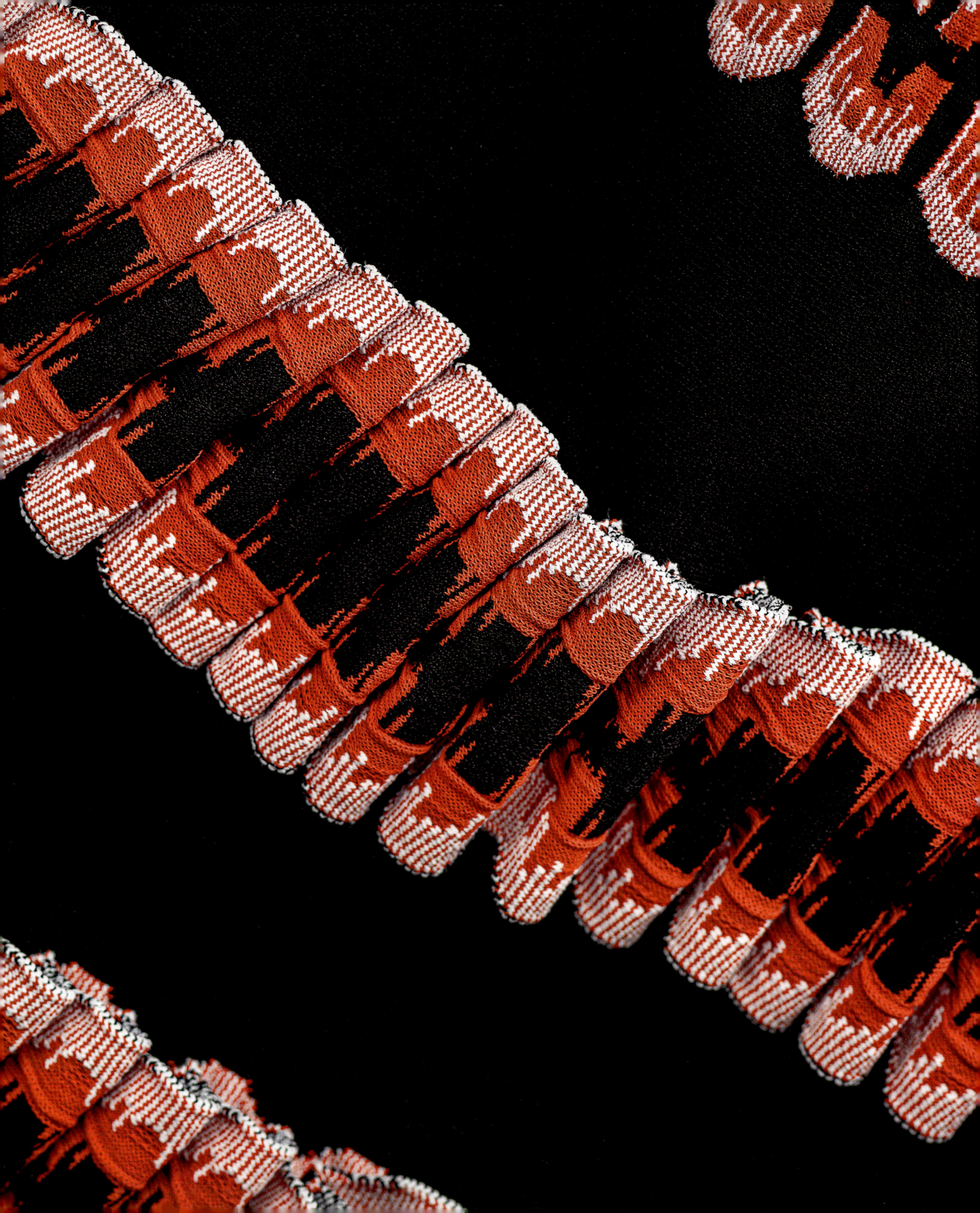

Jacquard viscose bolero developed for Alaïa,
2017 summer collection

"It was working on this garment that I finally realized that sometimes fashion follows the rules of engineering."

Lucy Shaw, Alaïa Knitwear designer

"Among ourselves we call this dress 'twisted table' because it was truly inspired by a piece of furniture."

Silvia Bocchese

Viscose dress with applique fringes
developed for Alaïa, 2022 summer collection

Dress with knitted crinoline developed for Alaïa,
2022 winter collection

Silk and rubber-effect polyurethan skirt
developed for Alaïa, 2023 winter collection

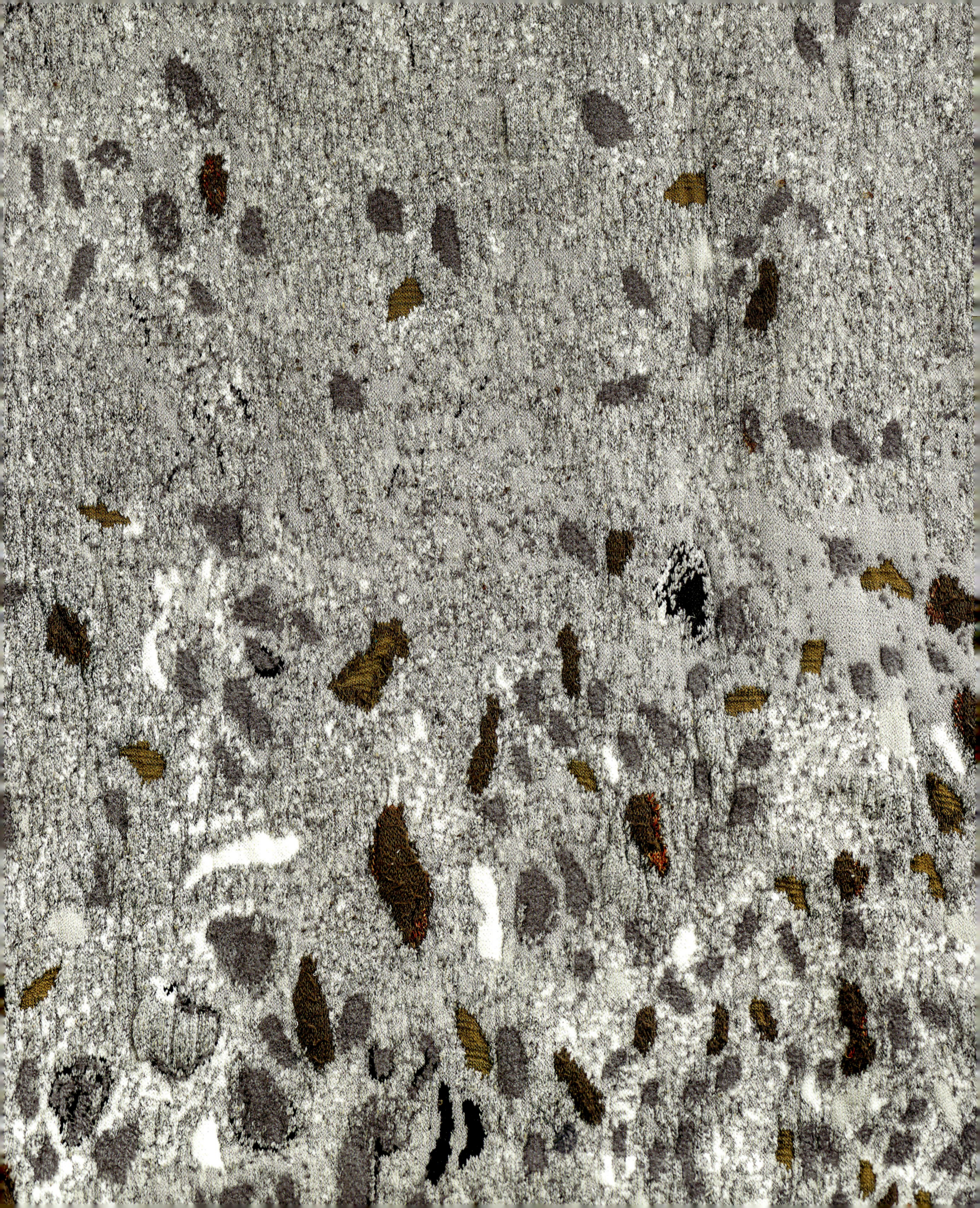

"Cement" jacquard dress developed for Alaïa,
2023 winter collection

"**This 'cement' jacquard was
designed by Pieter Mulier—
Alaïa's creative director
since 2021—inspired by the
floor of his house in Antwerp
where he hosted the show for
the 2023 winter collection.**"

Silvia Bocchese

Miles

The History of an Enterprise

Cristina Beltrami

1960

Inauguration of the new Giuseppe Bocchese & Figli plant in Via dell'Industria. Its state of the art looms were designed to ensure the production, "at industrial cost and with unvarying standards, of a textile that possessed all the qualities of something created by the hands of an artisan (while avoiding its defects)." (*Giuseppe Bocchese* n.d., p. 3)

1962

Seduced by the beauty and potential of spun silk, and with a touch of recklessness, "almost for a laugh" by her own admission, Silvia Bocchese opened a small workshop in Contra' Santa Chiara, in the historic city center of Vicenza: three workers on three machines, with the aim of producing a small number of models, especially white organzine turtlenecks for men to wear under their tuxedos like they did in American movies. She sold them to stores in Milan and Cortina. Silvia took care of the deliveries while her husband was in charge of the accounting, and Cleo, Silvia's mother, looked after the grandchildren. The Miles brand was officially born.

1967

Miles moved into a larger workshop in Via delle Grazie, still in Vicenza. This was where they received the visit of Lison Bonfils, a French model and designer who ordered a couple of

experimental sweaters: simple pieces in silk and in cashmere that she took to Paris, where they were immediately noticed by Hélène Gordon-Lazareff, a journalist and the founder of *Elle* magazine, which she had directed since 1945. The two sweaters were photographed for an editorial and their success led to the collaboration with Yves Saint Laurent.

1973

Giuseppe died in a car accident and Silvia found herself having to manage both family and business with the sole support of her mother, who never missed a day at the company until she was almost one hundred years old, always in her impeccable suit with white pants and gold buttons.

↘ Miles logo, designed in 1967

← The new Giuseppe Bocchese & Figli plant in the industrial area of Vicenza, circa 1960

↑ Detail of a warping machine with spools of dyed silk, 1960s

1975

Miles moved to Via del Progresso in the industrial area of Vicenza.

1980

In October, a terrible fire destroyed the plant, but with the few salvaged machines Miles resumed its activity in a workshop in Contra' Porti where the company already had a small warehouse.

1981

Beginning of the collaboration with Alaïa.

1982

A fashion show in New York marked the beginning of Alaïa's dizzying success, and Miles had to find a bigger headquarters.

1985

Miles moved into a former cloistered convent in the Colli Berici.

1986

Miles created the first stretch leggings for Alaïa. From that moment on, stretch yarns appeared in the collections of every brand.

1989

Beginning of the collaboration with Sonia Rykiel.

1995

The company moved into the Setificio Bocchese plant in Via dell'Industria, taking over and expanding the structure it still occupies to this day. They were licensed to produce and distribute Giorgio Armani's main men's and women's collections.

1996

Miles was licensed to produce and distribute Dolce & Gabbana's knitwear line.

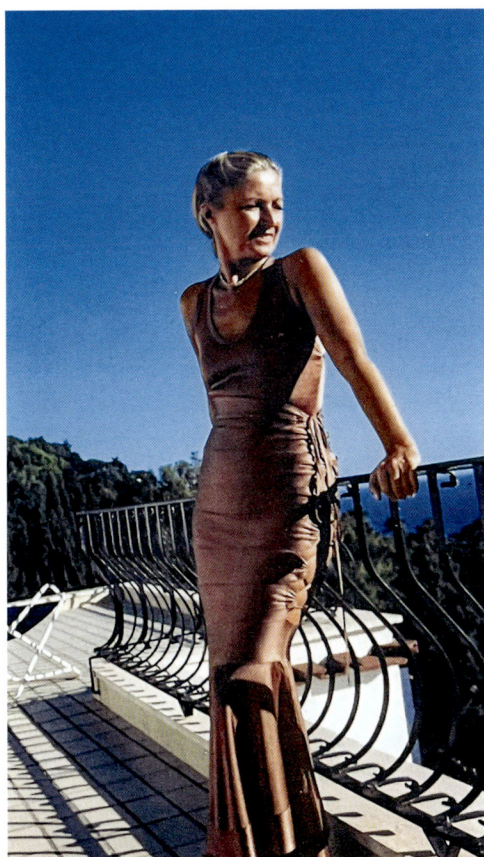

2001

Miles began a collaboration with From Somewhere, the brand designed by Orsola de Castro, a pioneer of sustainable fashion.

2008

Miles joined Comitato Leonardo – Italian Quality Committee, an association of entrepreneurs, artists, scientists and men of culture born in 1993 with the purpose of promoting Italy's image abroad.

2009

Miles created a number of experimental sculpture-like garments designed by Sandra Backlund.

2016

Miles initiated NeTTA – New Technology for Textile Application, a project focused on 3D printing and born from the cooperation with Lineapiù Italia, the Italian architecture firm PS Architettura, and Materialise. A number of garments produced using the innovative technique of 3D printing were presented at the show *Crafting the Future* curated by Franca Sozzani for MUDEC – Museo delle Culture in Milan.

2018

Silvia Bocchese was awarded the Talents du luxe et de la création prize in the Innovation category. Miles took part in the first edition of *Homo Faber* submitting some of their archive pieces, participating in the *Doppia firma* project, and presenting designs and photographs by Susanna Pozzoli.

↗ Silvia Bocchese in Capri, 1986

↑ "Little sketch done with love and respect by Sophie Théallet in Vicenza: Azzedine, Sylvia et Mirabelle"

Cristina Beltrami

2019

Miles received a prize in the Artisanal
Excellence category at the first edition
of the MF Supply Chain Awards devoted
to the most innovative businesses by the
Milano Fashion Global Summit.

2020

Sergio Mattarella, President of the
Italian Republic, nominated Silvia
Bocchese Cavaliere del Lavoro.

Present

The company has grown over the years
and in 2023 it had about two hundred
employees.
Today's headquarters occupy the
building designed in the early 1960s by
the architect Luigi Massoni for Setificio
Bocchese. The structure has been
completely renovated, significantly
reducing its environmental impact by
installing solar panels that meet the
energy requirement of the entire plant.
The original buildings from the 1960s
have been joined by a series of other

→ A dress from Alaïa's 2022 summer-fall
collection, inspired by Pablo Picasso's
ceramics

↘ The creation of a garment from Alaïa's
2022 summer-fall collection, inspired
by Pablo Picasso's ceramics

constructions and the surface they now
cover is about eleven thousand square
meters.
One of Miles's most significant assets
is surely its incredible archive of
prototypes, featuring over fifteen
thousand knitting stitches and over
thirty thousand garments created
for the most important brands in
international fashion and is unparalleled
for the number of pieces it includes but
even more so for the variety of knitwear
techniques represented.
The secret of Miles's many-decade-
long history and of their success can
be summed up in their perseverance in
the extreme quality of their production,
in an innovative technique and in the
cooperation with the big *maisons*:
these are the elements that led
to the achievements of this active
and prosperous company.

Bibliography

Giuseppe Bocchese n.d.
Giuseppe Bocchese & Figli. Vicenza: Litostampa Vajenti, n.d.

Schumacher 1973
E.F. Schumacher. *Small Is Beautiful*. New York: Harper Collins, 1973.

Bagnasco 1977
A. Bagnasco. *Tre Italie. La problematica territoriale dello sviluppo italiano*. Bologna: il Mulino, 1977.

Fuà and Zacchia 1983
G. Fuà and C. Zacchia, eds. *Industrializzazione senza fratture*. Bologna: il Mulino, 1983.

Bernardi 1987
U. Bernardi. *Paese Veneto. Dalla cultura contadina al capitalismo popolare*. Florence: Edizioni del Riccio, 1987.

Marini 1987
D. Marini. "La base sociale e l'insediamento territoriale." In *Tra religione e organizzazione. Il caso delle ACLI*, edited by I. Diamanti and E. Pace. Padova: Liviana Editrice.

"Quando il gioco si fa duro" 2006
"Quando il gioco si fa duro… il made in Italy entra in campo." In *Fashion*, 27 January, 2006, 15.

Stefani 2008
A. Stefani. "Come eravamo nel lavoro. Ecco il 'genio vicentino'." In *Il Giornale di Vicenza*, 20 May, 2008, 51.

Thaler and Sunstein 2008
R.H. Thaler and C.R. Sunstein. *Nudge. Improving Decisions About Health, Wealth and Happiness*. London: Penguin, 2008.

Giancotti 2009
M. Giancotti, ed. *Vite d'impresa. Storie di imprese che hanno cambiato il volto del vicentino*, n. 5. Vicenza: Camera di commercio industria artigianato agricoltura – Centro studi sull'impresa e sul patrimonio industriale, 2009.

Van Godtsenhoven and Dirix 2011
K. Van Godtsenhoven and E. Dirix, eds. *Unravel: Knitwear in Fashion*. Tielt: Lannoo, 2011.

Cinque 2012
F. Cinque. "Bocchese 1908. Un viaggio nella storia della seta italiana." In *My Where*, 14 December, 2012 (online).

Poletti 2012
F. Poletti with E. Dirix, eds. *Maglifico! 50 anni di straordinaria maglieria made in Italy*, exhibition catalog (Milan, Palazzo Morando, 21 June – 2 September, 2012). Milan: Skira, 2012.

Bolelli 2014
G. Bolelli. "Bocchese 1908 punta a USA e Nord Europa per il 2015." In *Fashion Network*, 21 October, 2014 (online).

Marini 2015
D. Marini, *Le Metamorfosi. Nord Est: un territorio come laboratorio*. Venice: Marsilio, 2015.

Frisa 2016
M.L. Frisa, ed. *Desire and Discipline: Designing Fashion at Iuav 2005-2015*. Venice: Marsilio, 2016.

Sozzani 2016
F. Sozzani, ed. *Crafting the Future. Storie di artigianalità e innovazione*, exhibition catalog (Milan, MUDEC, 21 September – 13 October, 2016). Milan: Camera nazionale della moda italiana, 2016.

d.l. 2018
d.l. "Bocchese presidente della sezione Moda di Confindustria Vicenza." In *FashionMagazine.it*, 4 October, 2018 (online).

"Silvia Stein Bocchese" 2018
"Silvia Stein Bocchese, presidente del Maglificio Miles, riceve il premio Talents de luxe et de la création." In *IndustriaVicentina*, 7 February, 2018 (online).

Favero 2020
G. Favero, "Marchi, Allegrini, Stein: i tre Cavalieri." In *Corriere del Veneto*, 31 May, 2020, 3.

Grazzini 2020
M. Grazzini. "La moda ha due nuovi Cavalieri del Lavoro." In *La Spola*, 3 June , 2020 (online).

"Il riconoscimento al valore di una donna" 2020
"Il riconoscimento al valore di una donna." In *Fashion Illustrated*, June, 2020 (online).

"Silvia Stein Bocchese" 2020
"Silvia Stein Bocchese è cavaliere del lavoro." In *Hub Style*, 3 June, 2020 (online).

Tomasoni 2020
S. Tomasoni. "Imprenditrice vicentina cavaliere del lavoro." In *Il Giornale di Vicenza*, 29 May, 2020, 19.

Pozzoli 2021
S. Pozzoli. *Venetian Way*.Venice – Genève: Marsilio – Michelangelo Foundation, 2021.

Sozzani and Saillard 2022
C. Sozzani and O. Saillard, eds. *Alaïa avant Alaïa*, exhibition catalog (Paris, 2022-2023). New York: Rizzoli International Publications, 2022.

"Maglificio Miles" 2022
"Maglificio Miles. Come scegliere i filati sostenibili. Il progetto Atlas." In *TechnoFashion*, February, 2022, 16.

Color reproduction and printing
Grafiche Antiga s.p.a., Crocetta del Montello (TV)
for Marsilio Arte® s.r.l., Venice